MASTERS RUNNING

5K TO HALF MARATHON

MASTERS RUNNING

5K TO HALF MARATHON

Optimised training for peak performance for 35 years and beyond

Jo Wilkinson

THE CROWOOD PRESS

Contents

Preface

My expertise in coaching Masters (those runners aged 35 years and over) is built on my personal experience as an elite athlete, along with my specialist knowledge from many years coaching some of the best runners in England in their forties, fifties and sixties. This book now brings all this expertise together to help you.

For ten years I was ranked in the British top ten over 5,000m, 10,000m, half marathon and marathon. On the track I represented England in the 2002 Commonwealth Games, finishing sixth in the 10,000m. On the road, I competed for Great Britain in the marathon at the 2010 European Championships as part of the Bronze Medal-winning team and finished in the top 20 in the London Marathon. All of this took place whilst juggling training as an elite athlete with my job as a social worker, the birth of two children, frequent house moves and numerous periods of lone parenting as my husband was repeatedly away for work.

Like so many people I didn't think I was good at sport at school, particularly when it came to anything involving a bat or ball. Then I discovered that even if I couldn't catch, I could run. I learned many lessons from my world-class coach, Alex Stanton, who also coached Paula Radcliffe, Olympian and marathon world record holder. But the most valuable lesson was to see the potential in everyone, whether they are world class or just want to run faster.

Now in my fifties I still love to run, but what motivates me most is coaching. It started with my first group, called Love Running, whose aim was to encourage more women to start running. Over time the name of the group evolved into The We Hate Running Collective. And yet, despite professing to hate running, that group of middle-aged women still turned up every week and gave it their best. Why? Because they found that with the right coaching, running was about more than just fitness, it was about fun, friendship and an enormous sense of achievement. Since then, I have coached many Masters runners who have set fast times, been ranked in the top ten for their age group and represented England Masters in 5k, 10k and half marathon.

Now as more men and women take up running later in life, many find (sometimes to their surprise) they are better than they thought too. My passion is sharing my knowledge, experience and expertise with them and you. I will coach you how to train, how to race and the importance of confidence and self-belief to performance. And most importantly, how to adapt your training to fit the demands in your life to be the best you can. Because you never know what you can do, until you try.

Introduction

Too many people are put off running because they think they are too old to start. Or they think it's too hard for them. Or they are worried it will damage their knees. This book is here to challenge all these myths and show you what you can achieve as a Masters runner. ('Masters' is the term now used for anyone who is 35 years or older.)

As more people in their forties, fifties, sixties and beyond take up running, it has become generally recognised that running is actually very good for you. Rather than cause damage to your joints, it promotes stronger muscles and bones. It strengthens your heart and helps with weight management. It helps manage the symptoms of the menopause. And it can bring positive benefits to your mental health.

Whilst many people take up running to lose weight, improve health or raise money for good causes, this book will show you that there is more to running as a Master than just cakes, calories or raising cash for charity.

Many Masters runners started running for all these reasons. Most of them had not done any sport since their schooldays. To start, they didn't run very far. They didn't run very fast. But over time they found they wanted to push themselves, run faster and be competitive too.

Katherine (56 years)

Katherine started running in her forties to raise money for the hospice that had cared for her Dad so well in his final days. At first, getting out for a run meant finding time, juggling childcare, work and other demands, but she found the commitment (and previously untapped fierce determination) to persevere, starting with just running 5k a couple of times each week to build her fitness.

From those humble beginnings to now, fifteen years later, Katherine has demonstrated that with the right structure and approach to training, you can improve beyond your expectations, setting outstanding personal best times of 18:59 for 5k, 38:46 for 10k and 1:23:34 for half marathon in her mid-fifties.

Sam (60 years)

At 39, Sam wanted to quit smoking so she started running. Short runs from her house to the local village shop and back again (with a break on the bench in-between). When she entered some races, she found she enjoyed being competitive and was better than she expected. But like many runners, she also started to pick up injuries and over time she had to find the balance between training and much-needed rest, especially as her job involved working long hours to manage cabin crew for a major airline.

She has now set new personal bests in her late fifties of 20:05 for 5k, 42:32 for 10k and 1:34:45 for half marathon, and represented Great Britain at the 2024 Masters World

Championships. When confronted by a well-meaning acquaintance at her 60th birthday party who said, 'Now you are a grandmother I assume you will be doing less running', Sam just smiled. Then she answered her by running one of her fastest half marathons three days later.

Hervé (48 years)

Hervé started running ten years ago as part of a health and fitness programme. He immediately loved its day-to-day health benefits, being able to walk upstairs without getting out of breath alongside significant weight loss. But even more he loved the calming, meditative effect of going for a long run, especially when balanced against his demanding role as a business leader in a global advisory company, involving long hours and international travel.

Now he is a passionate advocate for all the positives of running, whether it's just going for a daily run or challenging himself in races with personal best times of 24:53 for 5k, 55:22 for 10k and 2:07:13 for half marathon. Most importantly, wherever he may be in the world, Hervé always makes sure he finds time and somewhere to run.

John (68 years)

John started running in the army. Throughout his long career he took part in many sports but excelled most in running, in his younger days setting PBs of 68 minutes for half marathon and 2:40 for the marathon. Upon returning to civilian life he joined a running club, but as he grew older he went from one injury to the next.

What he needed was structure and consistency in his training, which he found again by adding strength work, warming up properly with planned rest and recovery. Whilst he can no longer beat his old times, John has run 21:49 for 5k, 45:51 for 10k and 1:34:56 for half marathon since turning 65. He has represented England Masters and admits he is as competitive as ever against his peers and aims to run long into his seventies and eighties.

Sam, Katherine, John and Hervé demonstrate that being older doesn't automatically mean being slower or not training as hard. But like them, it's important to acknowledge that our bodies change with age and running has to be balanced against other competing demands from work, family and life in general.

However, Sam, Katherine, John and Hervé also embody the physical and mental health benefits from running, reducing the likelihood of serious health problems, managing the impact of the menopause, enhancing confidence and providing a renewed sense of achievement that can so easily be lost as we age.

As a Masters runner, you are probably in your forties, fifties or sixties and fall into one of three groups:

- You are relatively new to running and would like to improve your performance over 5k to half marathon
- You used to run when you were younger and want to get started again, but have found that now you cannot just train like you did before without getting injured
- You have been a lifelong runner and want to keep running for as long as you can

This book is here to help you navigate training as a Masters runner. In the following chapters, we'll explore what you need to do to achieve your running goals and how to meet the challenges of training as you age, with structured plans that recognise your specific needs. This book will show you how to plan your training and peak for a specific race over 5k, 10k or half marathon, and how to deliver your best performance on the day.

To support your training and races, you'll also find advice on:

- The key concepts of recovery, rest and adaption that are fundamental to maximise training benefits
- How to individualise your training to suit your ability, lifestyle, work and family commitments
- The different factors you must consider based on your age and whether you are male or female
- The importance of strength work for older runners
- The crucial mental qualities of determination, confidence and resilience
- How to manage setbacks due to injury or illness

Many older runners struggle to identify with the label 'athlete'. We tend to think of 'athletes' as young, fit people in their prime of life and peak physical condition. And so I will use the term 'runner' throughout this book. However, I would argue that many older runners bring even more focus and determination to their running than most 'athletes', forged from their life experience.

Coaching Philosophy

Broadly speaking, my philosophy is that running should be something positive in your life, otherwise why do it? So, before we begin it's important to set out the core principles of coaching that underpin all of the advice in this book:

- Good coaching
- Balance between volume and intensity
- Rest, recovery and adaptation
- Health
- Positivity

Good Coaching

Good coaching is built on strong foundations of technical knowledge, expertise and experience whilst recognising what you do not know. For coaches of Masters runners, 'good coaching' means understanding how age impacts training principles, especially as most training knowledge and sports science research comes from working with athletes at the peak age of physical performance in the mid-twenties.

Unfortunately, most research has also tended to focus on males. This is partly because the female menstrual cycle creates uncertain and irregular baselines for research, with female runners broadly ignored until very recently. There is even less research into training principles for older women as they experience menopause. But gradually these gaps are being filled with a growing body of research into older runners.

Good coaching for masters (and all runners) means recognising gaps in experience and expertise alongside building knowledge over time.

Volume and Intensity

There is a strong correlation between volume (how much you run) and level of performance. In simple terms, the more you run, the fitter you will be and the faster you will run. Consistent, regular running over an extended period is key. This should be measured in years, not just months or weeks.

For Masters runners, however, it's not as easy as just doing more running week on week. Volume should be built incrementally and progressively, but not exponentially. Good training balances more with periods of consolidation and takes account of significant age-related changes to your body. This helps you to build better depth of fitness and avoid breakdown from injury or plateaus in performance from over-training.

A tipping point also comes when it isn't solely about running more, but the blend of pace and intensity at which you run also matters. The challenge for Masters runners is how to achieve this blend to get the results you want. This brings me to the next key concept.

Rest, Recovery and Adaptation

Adaptation is the body's physiological response to training stimuli. These include changes to the structure of muscles, tendons and bones, improved function of heart and lungs and more efficient energy systems. Contrary to popular misconception, adaptation takes place during the period of rest and recovery, not during training itself.

Successful Masters coaching means balancing training load with rest and recovery to maximise training benefits. If your training load is too high or too frequent, without sufficient rest and recovery, then adaptations will be lessened. As we age, muscles, bones and tendons lose strength and become less efficient at repair and regeneration. These changes can be more pronounced for female runners during the menopause. This makes older runners potentially more susceptible to injury if they do not incorporate appropriate rest and recovery.

Health

Perhaps the most important pillar in my coaching philosophy is that training must be built on good health. It may feel amazing to run faster than you have ever run before, but this is never worth compromising your long-term health and well-being. There is always some risk in training hard and pushing the limits. But good coaching should not recklessly push runners too hard for short-term gains.

Long-term health is even more important for Masters runners. The medical profession now widely recognises the positive health benefits of exercise, even for people with serious and enduring health conditions. However, it is important to always seek medical advice for any serious health condition and adapt training appropriately.

Equally importantly, we now recognise the menopause is a period of significant physical changes with an impact on mental health and well-being too. With the right approach, however, running during the perimenopause and post-menopause can help manage many of the symptoms and brings even more positive health benefits.

Positivity

Running should be something that makes you feel good. It can be a source of great confidence and sense of achievement for older runners. Running can also be highly effective in managing stress and maintaining mental well-being. It can give you a strong sense of identity and many, especially those who may feel lonely or excluded at times, find that it opens up membership to a community of like-minded people.

However, your sense of self-worth should not be solely reliant on running and results. Running should definitely not be punitive and negative. No one enjoys every run all of the time. There will be moments of pure elation and joy and there will be moments of deep disappointment and despair. Like life, running will be full of ups and downs, but broadly it should be a positive factor in your life.

To go back to where we started, whoever you are, whatever the reasons why you started running, however fast or not you may be, this book is here to show you what you can do, but it isn't a quick fix guide to running faster. Instead, it challenges you to stop thinking that time is ticking away, causing you to get sucked into searching for shortcuts that invariably end up in injury, illness or setbacks. Using the advice and training plans in this book will help you run faster but equally help you develop as a robust runner. So that even as you age you can still maintain form, fitness and consistency and, most importantly, continue to enjoy your running for many years to come.

PART I

GETTING STARTED

Life is for participating, not for spectating.

Kathrine Switzer, first woman to officially run the Boston Marathon

1 How to Get Started

We start with some basic principles of running: how fast to run and how to pace yourself. Then touch on mindset and finding determination, before finally considering where to run.

Before we get on to these let's dispel the big myth that to be a 'runner' you shouldn't stop or walk. There are a wide range of excellent Couch to 5k programmes available to help you get started if needed. These programmes gradually build up the volume of continuous running broken up by blocks of rest, recovery and walking. But taking some breaks is not just for beginners and even the most experienced runners will stop or walk on some of their runs, especially during some of the more challenging intervals sessions and workouts.

What pace to run seems like it should be simple. Newer runners often erroneously assume that you should set off as fast as you can then keep going for as long as you can. In practice this is an incredibly hard and painful way to run and not recommended. Instead, learning to pace yourself, which often means starting more slowly, helps you to run further and, ultimately, to run faster too.

But for every runner there comes a point when it gets hard and you need to push yourself. Being determined is a skill as much as a talent and something you can practise in training if you find it doesn't come naturally.

I literally just started by running from my house to the village shop, which is about three quarters of a mile. I'd sit on the bench and recover. And then I would jog back again. And that was just all I did.

Sam

How Fast to Run

Before you can think about how to pace yourself you need to consider how to monitor how fast you are running. There are a range of ways to do this with advantages and disadvantages to each. The most common methods are:

> *I listen to my feet. How would I know how fast I am running if I didn't have the thud, thud, thud of my feet?*
>
> Katherine

- Pace measured in minutes per kilometres (5:00/km)
- Rate of Perceived Exertion (RPE), usually on a scale of 1–10
- Heart rate (HR), measured in beats per minute (bpm) or percentage of maximum (85% max HR)
- Race pace, which means the pace you would run to cover the set race distance (5k pace or half marathon pace)
- Blood lactate levels measured in milli-moles per litre of blood (mmol/l)

Pace

Pace is measured as the time it takes you to run one kilometre (or one mile if you prefer to measure your running in miles). It can be the most objective and accurate method when recorded by stopwatch over an accurately measured distance.

Global Positioning System (GPS) watches use satellites to measure distance and pace as you run. They are very helpful although accuracy can vary subject to the strength of the GPS signal and environmental factors such as weather conditions, tall buildings or tree coverage.

As a coach I always advise runners to be pragmatic in sticking to a set pace in training. This is because your effort levels can be significantly affected by external factors such as temperature (hot or cold), wind, elevation (uphill or downhill), terrain (road, track or soft grass or mud), and internal factors such as illness, tiredness, stage of menstrual cycle or symptoms of the menopause. This means that using pace sometimes encourages you to run harder than you should just to hit a predetermined pace. Whilst measuring pace is very useful to monitor training, and is the key method used in this book, it should also be used with appropriate caution.

Rate of Perceived Exertion (RPE)

Rate of Perceived Exertion measures how fast you are running based on your perception of effort set against a descriptive scale. It is usually based on a scale of 1 to 10 (although it originates from the Borg Scale, named after its inventor Gunnar Borg, which went from a scale of 6 to 20).

RPE also incorporates the 'talk test'. This measures how many words you can say before you need to breathe. The harder you run, the heavier your breathing becomes and the more difficult it is to speak in full sentences. Rather than being 'unscientific', this has actually proved to be a highly accurate measure of effort and is used by many elite athletes and coaches.

Unlike objective pace, RPE helps you to tune into your body and encourages you to run at the right pace for you, based on how you feel on that day. However, the RPE scale can be subjective and less experienced runners may find it difficult to judge.

Keeping to a certain pace without looking at the watch too much is something I have learnt over time. Now I don't worry about it. I trust myself to know what feels right and I find I often have a much better pace than if I am checking my watch every kilometre.

Hervé

Heart Rate (HR) and Percentage Maximum Heart Rate

Heart rate is measured by using a chest strap, arm strap or wrist monitor (on a smart watch). Using heart rate to monitor training relies on accurate measurements. Chest straps and arm straps tend to be more accurate than wristwatch-based heart rate monitors as these can be affected by the tightness of the watch strap and skin tone.

RPE Score		Description
10	Maximum Effort	Maximum pace. Impossible to maintain effort for more than few seconds. Unable to talk
9	Extremely Hard Effort	Close to maximum pace. Difficult to maintain. Gasping for breath. Single words only
8	Very Hard Effort	Fast pace. Can sustain effort one or two minutes at most. Breathing heavily. Single words
7	Good Effort	Fast pace. Breathing heavily. Able to sustain for several minutes. Two or three words only
6	Medium Effort	Faster pace but comfortable to maintain for longer period. Breathing significantly increased. Able to say short sentences
5	Moderate Effort	Pace requires conscious effort but able to hold for reasonable period of time. Breathing increased from normal. Able to speak in sentences
4	Comfortable Effort	Comfortable pace. Able to sustain effort for significant period of time. Increased breathing rate from normal but can hold conversation
3	Light Effort	Easy pace or jog. Able to maintain for extended period of time. Breathing slightly increased but able to maintain full conversation
2	Very Light Effort	Slow jog or fast walk. Able to hold full conversation
1	Minimal Effort	Very easy walk. Minimal effort required. Breathing not significantly increased from rest

Effective use of heart rate to monitor your runs also requires accurate assessment of your individual maximum heart rate and calculation of your individual zones. Generic formulas are available, but they are based on broad factors such as age and gender and tend to have a large margin of error.

Alternatively, you can determine your individual maximum heart rate and training zones by conducting your own field test or visiting a sports science laboratory for physiology testing. Field tests for maximum heart rate are often physically and psychologically difficult to perform, especially for less experienced runners. Physiology testing is much more accurate but needs to be done in a specialist laboratory and can be expensive.

Heart rate may also be affected by a range of factors such as fatigue, illness, stress and weather conditions. This means, as with methods using GPS and pace, you need to exercise a similar degree of caution in practice.

Race Pace

Race pace describes the pace at which you would currently run that distance. If your current 5k time is 25:00 then your 5k pace is 5:00/km. The advantage of race pace is that it is individual to each runner and their current ability and is familiar and relatable for most runners.

One common mistake is to set 'race pace' at your personal best time or target time rather than current fitness. Target time must be realistic and as a coach I often use the term 'training race pace', which allows pace to be more flexible subject to current fitness, stage of training and goals.

Blood Lactate Levels

Lactate is a substance produced in the body from the process of creating energy. The role of lactate is discussed in more detail in Chapter 6. Effort levels can be monitored by taking a small sample of blood and measuring the lactate concentration in millimoles per litre of blood (mmol/l). At rest lactate levels are usually approximately 1–2mmol/l. As intensity of exercise increases the lactate concentration also increases.

Measuring blood lactate levels provides a very accurate assessment of the intensity of exercise and is commonly used by elite athletes. However, it requires specialist equipment and the need to take blood can be intrusive and disruptive as it requires the runner to stop exercising to take regular blood samples. This means it is not generally practical for most runners in day-to-day training.

How to Pace Yourself

Knowing how fast you are running helps you to pace yourself in training and races. Pacing yourself means managing the distribution of effort over the duration or distance required. Contrary to some expectations, setting off at a pace you can maintain for the whole distance helps you run significantly faster in races, as well as maximises the training benefits from your running.

Learning how to pace yourself is an important skill for all runners. Some are naturally better at it than others, but every runner can improve with practice, so discipline and pace judgement should form a regular part of your training.

How Pacing Yourself Makes You Faster

It is now proven that, across all abilities, the fastest runners tend to run the most evenly paced races. Those runners who go off too fast, slow down more in the latter stages and perform worse in comparison to their best times. This has been demonstrated by extensive analysis of world records. But it doesn't just apply to elite athletes. The benefit of even pacing is backed up by large-scale analysis of running data from thousands of everyday runners on running apps.

The advantages of even pacing are also supported by the growing body of sport science research that explains the complex physiological reasons behind good pacing. In relatively simple terms, if runners set off too fast in relation to their ability they will become overwhelmed by changes in key metabolic markers. This will force them to succumb to fatigue and slow down disproportionately. Whilst the science is complicated, the message is clear. Even pacing makes you faster.

Pace Judgement in Training and Intervals Sessions

'Maximum training benefits for minimum training load' is one of my (many) favourite coaching expressions. Pacing yourself in training is as important as pacing yourself in races to get the most from your running.

Many inexperienced runners believe that the best way to get faster is to run intervals sessions as hard as they can from the start. However, in the majority of workouts this is counterproductive and means either the

Models of Pacing in Endurance

Pacing Strategy	Description	Applications
Positive	The pace starts fast and slows down as the race progresses	800m Cross-country Inexperienced runners
Even	The pace is relatively even throughout the race	Time trials World records All race distances from 800m to marathon
Negative	The pace starts slower and gradually gets faster as the race progresses.	Elite 5,000m or 10,000m track races Competitive 5k or 10k road races Marathon
Mixed	The pace may go up or down throughout the race	Championship 5,000m or 10,000m track races Half marathon

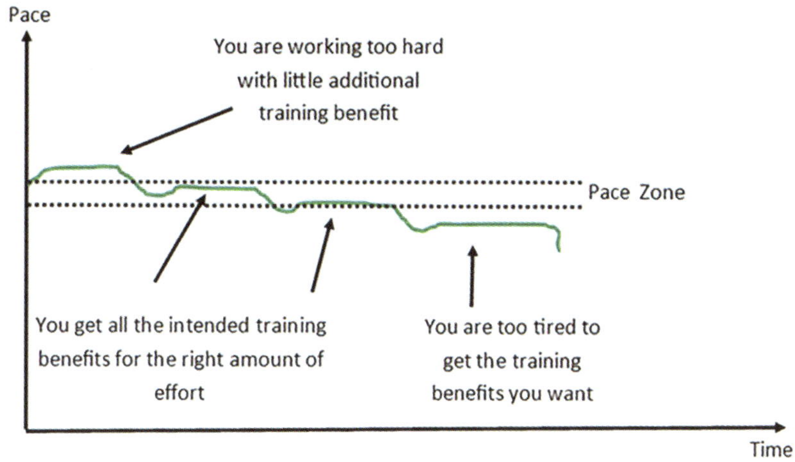

Training benefits from pace judgement in intervals sessions.

session has to be cut short or the last few intervals end up significantly slower.

In chapters 6 and 7 we will discuss the importance of training at certain key physiological intensities such as easy aerobic pace, lactate threshold and VO_2 max. To get the most training benefits, intervals should be evenly paced across the whole session. Training that strays too far above or below these intensities starts to limit the potential fitness gains. It also increases the risk of injury from pushing too hard on overly and unnecessarily fatigued muscles.

How to Develop Determination

How do you keep going when your legs are dying, your lungs are burning and the little voice inside your head is screaming at you to stop?

Years of experience as an athlete and coach have shown me that the mental aspect of running is as important as the physical side. Some runners have an innate ability to push themselves, but others find it more difficult to step out of their comfort zone. However, like all skills, you can improve your ability to push yourself and be determined

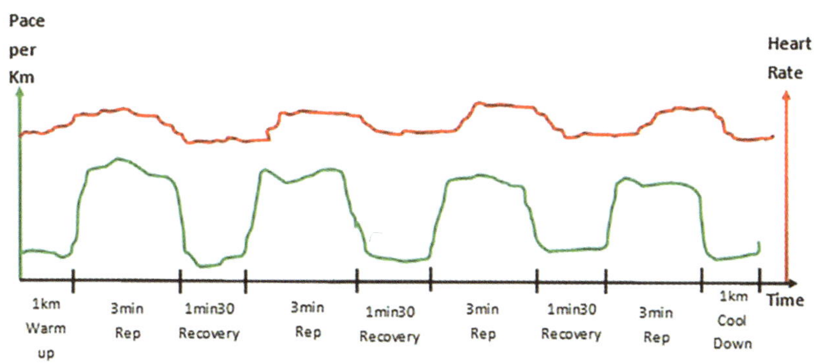

How to pace intervals sessions.

with focused practice in training and these are some common strategies and techniques.

Self-talk is our inner dialogue. Positive self-talk is a key skill to learn for all runners and lies behind most of these strategies. It involves consciously responding to any negative thoughts with positive statements. These might include mantras or motivational statements. They might include specific reminders or instructions at certain stages in the race such as 'run tall' or 'push on at 3k'. The more you practise positive self-talk, the more this will become second nature to you.

Reward

One of the most common techniques is to promise yourself a reward for your determination. This might be something tangible: cake, beer, new trainers. Or it might be the sense of achievement and satisfaction when you succeed.

Mantras

Mantras are highly effective. They are short, repeatable phrases that can help distract you from the discomfort and simultaneously focus you on what you need to do to achieve your desired outcome.

At the Masters World Championship I was finding it tough. So I told myself 'Come on Sam! You're doing OK. You're nearly 60 so it's OK'. Then I was overtaken by a 75-year-old woman. So my next conversation with myself was me swearing at myself and telling myself to get a grip and run faster!

Sam

Over time I have found myself adopting your mantra 'Come on Joanna!' to help me in my training too. It spurs me on and reminds of your support when I need it most.

Katherine

They might be motivational or instructional or just something that means something to you.

Breaking it down

Another good technique can be to mentally break down your run or workout into more manageable blocks. In practice this might be another two minutes, the next tree or running to the next visual landmark.

This is called 'chunking' and is one of the techniques favoured by top sports psychologist Josephine Perry and described in her 2019 book *Performing under Pressure*: 'It is used by athletes to help them feel whatever is ahead of them is more manageable by breaking down large, and often scary, events or competitions into bite sized things that are easier to face.'

Distraction

Distraction is another useful technique and many runners listen to music or podcasts to distract them from discomfort as they run. Other forms of distraction include singing to yourself or counting.

However, the distraction should not be so great that it distracts you from the necessary effort to reach your goal.

Reality checks

The definition of determination is to keep trying when something is difficult. It's often worth reminding yourself that what you are doing feels hard because it is hard. By its very definition, running a personal best means running faster than you have ever run before. This reality check can focus your mind on the need for determination when you may start to feel discouraged.

Developing resilience

Don't let the setbacks set you back. At times running is hard and interruptions from illness or injury can never be fully eliminated. Likewise, performance in races or training often relies on things that you cannot control, such as the performance of other runners and external factors such as weather. Resilience is the ability to accept that things do not always go to plan. Learn from setbacks and continue to strive for success.

Focus on consistency

The biggest misconception in running is the belief that good runners never have bad sessions. It's not true. The key to successful running is consistency. You will get fitter from stacking one consistent session or run on top of another than you will from one or two outstanding runs. This means if you give up on too many sessions because they aren't going well, you start to lose the essential consistency in your training programme and overall fitness will suffer more.

Change the goal

Rather than get disheartened or walk away from the session, sometimes you can change the goal. Some days that might mean taking some walking breaks on your run, adding some extra recovery between intervals, or splitting each repeat into two. Change the goal to just finishing the session, not just hitting your target pace, and build the consistency that is so important.

Where to Run

The last thing to consider as you get started is where to run. Most of the time the choice should be straightforward and based on convenience and time available. You put on your trainers, open the front door and start running. But if you have time to be flexible then it's useful to consider what different running surfaces might bring to your running and training.

Road/Tarmac

From a practical perspective road is often the most convenient surface for training. Good quality road, tarmac or pavement is good for all types of runs and especially as you move on to intervals sessions.

The main advantage of road is specificity. If your goal is 5k, 10k or half marathon then a good proportion of your running should be on road. Ideally look for routes with as few road crossings as possible or, even better, traffic-free roads or paths in parks to minimise interruptions. From a safety perspective street lighting is important for running in the dark.

The downside is that road can be a very hard surface, which puts greater load from repeated impact on your body. Therefore it is important to ensure your trainers have a good degree of cushioning and, if possible, mix road with softer surfaces for some of your runs.

Grass

Grass is an excellent surface for all types of training and runs. Good quality grass that is short and flat with no holes is great for easy runs or fast intervals sessions. Longer or more uneven grass may be more suitable just for easy runs.

The advantage of grass is that it puts less impact on joints, muscles and tendons. The disadvantage is that the soft and uneven surface makes it harder to run faster and, in wet conditions, grass may become slippery or muddy.

Trail

Trail tends to refer to more technical terrains such as stony and rocky paths, gravel, mud, tree roots, steep hills and overgrown foliage. Trail can be an excellent surface for easy runs where there is no pressure on pace and the goal is time on feet. However, more technical trail routes are not appropriate for intervals or mixed pace workouts where you are targeting specific pace and effort.

Track

An athletics track can be an excellent place to train. It provides an accurately measured, uniform, flat surface, which is ideal for focusing on pace and speed in intervals sessions.

In addition to the training benefits, most tracks also provide safe locations to run that are floodlit in the dark and usually free from potential hazards and interruptions such as dogs, pedestrians, cyclists and traffic.

However, newer runners may be put off because they are unfamiliar with aspects of running on the track, so here is a basic introduction to running on the track.

Basic Track Information

One lap of the track on the inside lane is 400m. Each outer lane adds approximately 2 metres to each lap. The start and finish of each lap is usually marked by a thick white line across the track and large white numbers. Every 100m is marked by a white horizontal line across each lane. There are also numerous other lines in different colours that denote hurdles and relay points, but that are not relevant for endurance so you can broadly ignore all of them.

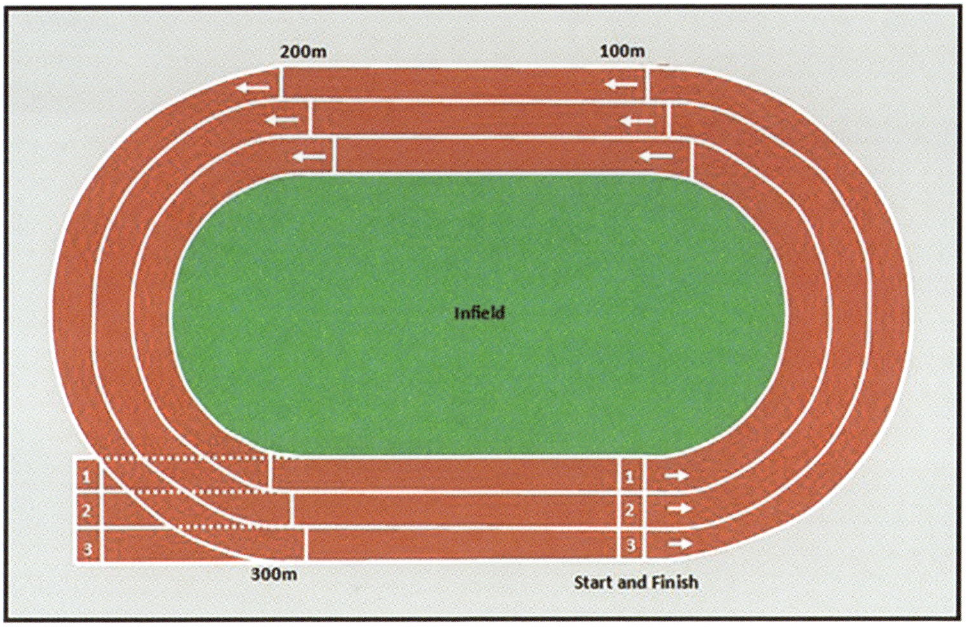

Key features of an athletics track. Each lap of the track is 400m. You should always run anti-clockwise around the track in lane 1.

Track Etiquette and Track Rules

You should always run anticlockwise around the track. Check individual facility rules about lane usage. In general, on most tracks the inside lane is used for intervals, training sessions and faster running and the outer lanes for jogging, recovery, warm up or cool down.

Always look before you step onto the track. Stepping in front of another runner is disruptive and potentially dangerous. In general, when you want to stop, step onto the inside of the track to avoid impeding other runners behind you.

You should never cross the grass infield as this is highly dangerous when it is being used for throwing events.

Track Footwear

Spikes are specific track shoes with small metal spikes in the sole, which help grip the track. They are usually for track races and sometimes for use in training. However, they provide little cushioning and may cause injury if you use them too often. For most runners, everyday trainers are more appropriate as they provide better cushioning. Even as an elite athlete who regularly competed on the track, most of my track sessions were done in trainers to minimise the risk of injury.

2 Running Technique for Masters

For most runners, how you think about running probably focuses more on 'how fast to run' than 'how to run'. As age takes hold, there is a number of commonly recognised changes to running technique arising from changes in muscle strength, tendon stiffness and mobility. However, the good news is that working on running drills, movement exercises and strength consistently over time will keep you running more smoothly and faster for longer.

Why is Running Technique Important for Masters?

How you run is important for several key reasons.

- Address age-related changes in running technique
- Minimise risk of injury
- Potential improvement in performance

To run, you propel yourself forwards by applying biomechanical force through the body to the ground. The more efficiently and effectively you can apply that force (your running technique) the more economically you move (which means it costs you less energy) and the faster you can run. Perhaps even more importantly, the best way to improve performance is to avoid repeated interruptions from injury, which can be helped by addressing poor running technique.

Most injuries arise when your muscles, tendons and bones are not strong or stable enough to absorb and control the repetitive forces from running. The risk of injury is further compounded by our body's natural tendency to compensate for weaknesses by creating alternative (often dysfunctional) movement patterns. These protect the weak

> *Now I am older goodness knows what is going on inside as these days I have to work so hard just to propel myself along!*
>
> John

Ground contact.

Mid stance.

Toe off.

Swing or flight phase.

tissues by directing forces onto other muscles, tendons or bones. Unfortunately, if these alternative tissues are also not strong enough then you end up with even further breakdown and injury.

Unfortunately for Masters runners, age-related decline in the strength and function of muscles and tendons starts to affect how you move and the force you can generate. One of the few studies of well-trained older runners (rather than comparing sedentary individuals) was published by Ceri Diss and others as 'Stance limb kinetics of older male athletes endurance running performance' in *Sports Biomechanics* (2015). It provides excellent insights into key changes in running technique. They identified a range of differences including shortened stride length, increased ground contact time, reduced trajectory in flight and reduced ankle mobility in the older runners.

But before you lose heart, there is good evidence to suggest that these issues can be significantly improved with regular and targeted strength and mobility work. Even more positively, almost all studies of older runners have shown that they have better health and mobility than those who don't do any exercise.

What is Good Running Technique?

There are four key stages in the running cycle:

- Ground contact
- Mid stance
- Toe off
- Swing or flight phase

Ground Contact

This is the point when the foot first makes contact with the ground. The shin should be vertical to the ground and the foot should land close to the hips. Ideally the foot has toes pulled up towards the shin (dorsiflexed) and lands on the midfoot to forefoot rather than heel or toes. This allows the Achilles tendon to act like an elastic band that absorbs energy as it stretches on ground contact. This energy is then explosively released to propel you forwards as the foot leaves the ground. This process is known as the stretch-shortening cycle.

Common Issues

Overstriding occurs when the foot lands further in front of the hips and the shin is significantly angled. Overstriding creates potentially damaging braking forces that slow your running stride and increase the risk of injury.

The foot should point forwards as it makes contact. If it is turned inwards or outwards it is usually a sign of limited range of movement in the ankle. This angling of the foot can then potentially cause damaging rotational forces through the ankle, lower leg and knee.

Elastic energy from the stretch-shortening cycle is maximised by speed of ground contact. This means if you have poor ankle mobility or extended ground contact then the calf muscles must work harder instead.

Ground contact. Ideally your foot should land closer to your hips, with the shin vertical to the ground.

Mid Stance

Mid stance is when the foot is in contact with the ground and the centre of mass is over the foot. The body should be stable with minimal forwards or backwards lean and no excessive rotation. The stance foot should be pointing forwards with no inwards roll or collapse. The glutes should stabilise the stance leg with the pelvis level and the knee aligned with the foot rather than falling inwards.

Arms should be bent at approximately 90 degrees at the elbow and should swing backwards and forwards without crossing the midline of the body. Elbows should not be excessively flared or pointing outwards as they move backwards.

Common Issues

Lack of stability in either the foot or glutes causes downwards collapse of the body and unwanted extra rotation through the hips and trunk. This can cause the knee to drift inwards putting pressure on the knee tendons. If the glutes are weak then the pelvis may drop to one side. This means the other knee cannot swing through smoothly in preparation for the next step. Throwing one arm out to the side can often be evidence of the body's natural attempt to counterbalance excessive rotation elsewhere.

Mid stance: the centre of mass is over the stance foot. Your pelvis should be level and neither knee trift inwards.

Toe Off

Toe off is the phase as the foot leaves the ground. Maximum power is created by fully straightening through the hip, knee and ankle (known as triple extension) as the foot pushes off against the ground. The other knee is driven forwards ready for the next ground contact.

Common Issues

Poor mobility in the hip, knee or ankle may limit the ability to fully straighten during toe off, which limits the application of power. Weak hip flexors mean the other knee cannot be pulled through with sufficient power to be in the best position for the next ground contact. This can result in scuffing the ground with the swing leg.

Swing or Flight Phase

During this phase neither foot is in contact with the ground and the legs are reorganised ready for the next ground contact.

As the foot leaves the ground the knee starts to swing through under the body. At the same time the shin of the other leg is swung down ready to make ground contact again.

Common Issues

Lack of mobility, strength and power mean that the swing or flight stage may be shortened or non-existent. This means the legs cannot be moved efficiently into the correct position ready to start the running cycle again.

Toe off. Maximum power is generated when the hip, knee and ankle are fully extended (straightened) as the foot pushes off from the ground.

Swing or flight phase. As your foot leaves the ground the knee should swing under the body, ready for the next ground contact.

Basic Running Positions and Movement Patterns

'Quality over quantity' is the guiding mantra for this chapter. Good running technique relies on the foundations of good basic running positions and movement patterns. So whilst these initial exercises might seem unimportant or unexciting, it is fundamentally important to be able to master these basic movements before you move onto more complex running drills and strength exercises.

The key basic movements for running are these:

- Posture
- Squat
- Lunge
- Hinge
- Upper body rotation
- High knee position

Posture.

Head: Chin should be level with no significant tilt of the head either forwards or backwards.

Shoulders: Relaxed position. Slightly pulled back. Not raised to the ears, hunched or rounded.

Trunk: Upright posture. Lifting up through the trunk. Not bent forwards or backwards and not leaning to either side.

Pelvis: Tucked under trunk in neutral position with no tilt forwards. Not slumped through the pelvis and hips. Pelvis remains level and does not drop to one side.

Posture

Let's start with what makes good posture. Good posture is essential to enable you to effectively and efficiently direct force downwards towards the ground to propel you forwards and minimise energy leakage. Energy leakage is when you lose energy either making or trying to control unnecessary and unwanted movements (often over-rotation) during running.

As we get older, weakened postural muscles in the abdomen and lower back, along with restricted mobility in key joints, can change and weaken posture. A sedentary lifestyle or long periods of sitting or driving create further weakness and tightness in the hips and glutes, which can impact the ability to stand fully upright.

Squat

Squats require good mobility in your upper back, hips, knees and ankles. During squats you move from triple extension (straightened through the hip, knee and ankle) into triple flexion (bent at the hip, knee and ankle)

Squat.

Feet should be positioned slightly wider than shoulder width with toes turned slightly outwards.

Weight should be maintained through the whole foot (not tipping onto toes or heels) and feet should remain flat on the floor throughout.

Lower body into squat position by pushing hips backwards.

Knees should remain aligned with toes and not drift inwards.

Trunk should remain neutral.

Lower until thighs parallel with the ground or trunk cannot remain relatively upright or feet cannot remain flat.

and back again. This pattern of triple extension to triple flexion is fundamental to running. In addition, the ability to perform a good squat enables you to progress onto a range of important strength exercises.

Lunge

Lunges require similar mobility to squats through hips, knees and ankles as well as creating additional hip extension (straightening) through the rear leg. Lunges are important single leg exercises and help to address strength and mobility imbalance between legs.

Lunge.
Step forwards with one leg ensuring that as you step forwards you start to lower towards the ground with rear leg.
The front leg should have thigh parallel to the ground with shin in vertical position and foot flat on the ground.
Knee of front leg should remain aligned with foot and not drift inwards.
Both feet should be pointing forwards and not turned outwards.
Knee of rear leg should be just above the ground.
Trunk should remain upright and not lean forwards or to the side.

Hinge.
Slightly soften knees and allow them to drift forwards if necessary during the hinge.
Tighten abdominal muscles and keep trunk neutral throughout.
Bend over from hips by pushing hips backwards whilst maintaining gently softened knees, but not full knee bend.

Hinge

Hinges require good mobility in hips. They are often restricted by length and mobility in hamstrings. Hinging is important to enable you to progress on to deadlifts and other strength exercises.

Upper body rotation.
Stand upright with arms crossed on chest and feet shoulder width apart.
Keep legs, pelvis and hips fixed.
Rotate upper body to one side.
Return to the centre and rotate to the opposite direction.

Upper Body Rotation

Running relies on some degree of counterrotation whereby the shoulders slightly rotate in one direction whilst the hips rotate in the opposite direction. Therefore a good range of movement through the upper and lower back, as well as the hips, is important to run.

High knee position.
Stand upright on one leg with foot flat on the floor and fully straightened through the knee and hip
Lift the other leg so that there are 90 degree angles at the hip, knee and ankle, and foot is in dorsiflexed position (toe up).
Keep trunk upright and do not lean backwards or sideways.

High Knee Position

The high knee position is one of the key movement patterns in running and running drills. It repeats the pattern of triple extension to triple flexion that is so fundamental to how to run.

Mobility Exercises and Walking Drills

The next step (quite literally) is to put these basic running positions into practice with mobility and walking drills. These work on the key elements that are most important for Masters runners: stability, posture, bending and straightening at the hip (flexion and extension), engagement of the glutes and ankle mobility.

Unless otherwise stated, perform each drill over 20 metres and repeat three times.

Toe Taps

Toe taps work on ankle mobility through the full range of movement from dorsiflexion (toes up) to plantarflexion (toes down). They also help to strengthen calf and shin muscles.

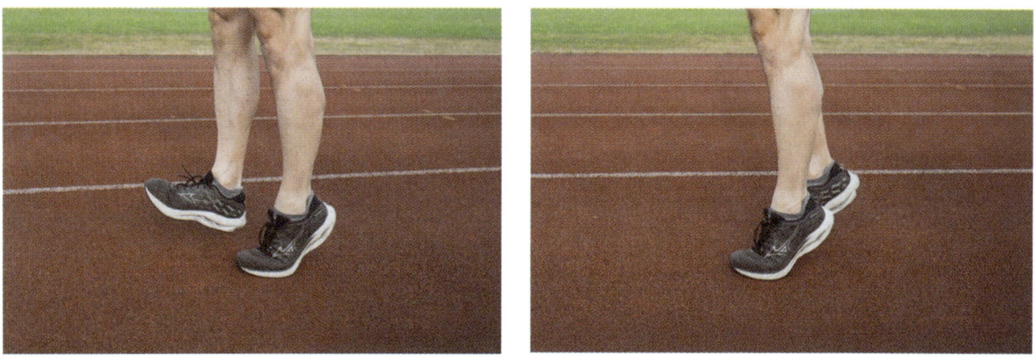

Toe taps.

1. Stand on tiptoes.
2. Take small steps forward (no more than one foot length for each step).
3. On each step flex your toes up towards your shin, then actively tap your toes down on the ground.
4. Keep heels elevated throughout the drill.

Heel walks.

1. Stand on heels with toes pulled up towards the shin.
2. Take small steps forwards, maintaining this position throughout.

Foot to toe rolls (ankling).
1. As you step forwards land on flat foot with equal ground contact between heel and forefoot.
2. Deliberately and with control and stability push up on to toe, ensuring that weight remains evenly spread across the forefoot from big toe to outer toes.
3. Take small steps forward, repeating this movement.

Heel Walks

Heel walks help to strengthen the muscles in the shin that control dorsiflexion of the ankle (toes up). They also work to mobilise and stretch the calf muscles.

Foot to Toe Rolls (ankling)

Foot to toe rolls work the ankle through its range of movement from dorsiflexion (toes pulled up) to plantarflexion (toes pointed down). It also works to strengthen the calf and shin muscles and improve foot stability.

High Knee Walk (overleaf)

High knee walks focus on good trunk control and stability, whilst moving each leg through triple extension (fully straightened at the hip, knee and ankle) into triple flexion (bent to 90 degrees at hip, knee and ankle). This drill also challenges the hip flexors to work effectively to lift the knee without any backwards lean to compensate for any weakness, poor mobility or shortened length.

Lunge Walks (overleaf)

Lunge walks engage the glutes to stabilise the knee and avoid inward collapse. They also support good trunk control to maintain upright posture and encourage full extension through the hip in the rear leg.

High knee walk.

1. Start with good posture (head level, relaxed shoulders, gently tighten trunk muscles and tuck pelvis under body).
2. Lift one knee so that the quad is horizontal to the ground, the shin is vertical and the foot is dorsiflexed with toes pulled up towards the shin. There should be 90-degree angles at the hip, knee and ankle joint.
3. The knee and hip should be fully straightened on the standing leg. Do not allow pelvis to tilt forwards to compensate for any lack of mobility or shortened length in the hip flexor.
4. Ensure you maintain a strong upright posture throughout and do not lean back to compensate for any weakness in hip flexors.
5. Take small steps and ensure you plant your foot on the mid to forefoot just in front of the centre of mass.

Lunge walks.

1. Step forwards with one leg, ensuring you plant foot onto mid to forefoot.
2. Tighten trunk muscles to keep pelvis in neutral position and do not allow it to tilt forwards at any point.
3. Lower into the lunge position whilst keeping trunk upright and ensuring you maintain stability and control.
4. Front shin remains vertical, front knee is aligned over the outer toes and the rear knee bends approximately 90 degrees towards the floor.
5. Push off with front foot and lift trunk upwards to take next step forward onto other foot.
6. Repeat as above.

Reverse lunge to high knee.

1. Step backwards and lower into lunge position.
2. Front shin remains vertical, front knee is aligned over the toes and the rear knee bends approximately 90 degrees towards the floor.
3. Maintain upright trunk position and engage abdominal muscles.
4. Push off through front foot and lift trunk whilst swinging rear leg through into high knee position.
5. In high knee position quad is horizontal, shin is vertical and foot is dorsiflexed with toes pulled up towards the shin to make 90-degree angles at the hip, knee and ankle joints.
6. On the standing leg glutes should be engaged to hold pelvis in neutral position and the knee and hip should be fully extended (straightened).
7. Ensure you maintain a strong upright posture throughout and do not lean back to compensate for weak hip flexors in high knee or allow pelvis to tilt forwards in lunge.
8. Step back and repeat on same leg for five repeats on each leg.

Reverse Lunge to High Knee

This drill builds on both high knee walks and lunges. It moves the glutes and the hip flexors through their full range of movement and function. As you step back into the lunge, the glutes on the stance leg should be engaged to stabilise the knee and prevent any downwards or inwards collapse of the knee, which would put undue pressure on the knee joint. As you step up into the high knee position the glutes then work to push the hips forwards. This exercise also helps mobilise the hips from extension (straightened or standing upright) into flexion (bent). It also works the hip flexors to swing the knee forwards into the high knee position similar to the running stride.

Hamstring Sweeps

Hamstring sweeps require you to hinge at the hips and help to mobilise hamstrings and lower back.

Hamstring sweeps.

1. Take small step forwards with front leg straight and place heel of front foot on floor with toes turned upwards.
2. Gently hinge at hips, moving them backwards as you lower trunk.
3. Swing arms through from behind body to in front.
4. Stand upright and take next step.

Dribbles.
1. Ensure foot lands on mid to forefoot and toe is kept up (dorsiflexed) throughout.
2. Bring each foot up over the ankle in a circular motion on each step.
3. Keep each step small (approx. one foot length on each step).
4. Keep trunk upright throughout and do not look down or lean forwards.

Running Drills

Finally, we move from walking to running. Running drills are dynamic exercises that build on the movement patterns you have already practised with the emphasis now on speed of movement and ground contact time, alongside good stability and posture.

Dribbles

Dribbles are small but exaggerated running steps in which the foot should be lifted no higher than just above ankle height and the foot is kept dorsiflexed (toe up) throughout.

Scissor Kicks

Scissor kicks work on good ground contact and reactivity. They are straight leg runs which encourage use of the glutes and hamstrings.

High Knee Drills

High knee drills are dynamic versions of high knee walks. Similar technical points apply, except the speed is increased so that it's closer to the running action with a period of flight between each step.

Scissor kicks.
1. Keeping the legs straight throughout, aim to gently kick legs forwards and pull backwards before foot is planted.
2. Foot should land in small steps just in front of the centre of mass
3. Foot should be kept in dorsiflexed position with toes up and foot planted on mid to forefoot.
4. Trunk should be kept upright throughout.

High knee drills.
1. Start with good posture (head level, relaxed shoulders and pelvis tucked under body).
2. Lift one knee so that the quad is horizontal to the ground, shin is vertical and foot is dorsiflexed with toes pulled up towards the shin to make 90-degree angles at the hip, knee and ankle.
3. The knee and hip should be fully extended (straightened) on the standing leg.
4. Foot should land on mid to forefoot just in front of centre of mass.
5. Ensure you maintain a strong upright posture throughout and do not lean back to compensate for weak hip flexors.
6. Aim for short ground contact time on each step.

Heel Kicks

Heel kicks are often wrongly described as 'butt kicks'. In this drill the aim is to emphasise good leg recovery through the swing phase to ensure the lower leg and foot are brought through into the right position ready to make the next ground contact.

Pogo Jumps

Pogo jumps technically fall under the category of plyometric exercises rather than running drills. However, they are excellent to encourage shorter ground contact time and to work the ankles and muscles of the lower leg.

Heel kicks.
1. As you take each step bend your knee and bring your heel up to directly under your centre of mass. Heel should not flick up behind you or hit your glutes.
2. Keep foot dorsiflexed throughout so that foot is in good position for next ground contact
3. Land on mid to forefoot and aim to minimise ground contact time.
4. Focus on speed of movement of each heel kick rather than speed of travel across the ground.

Pogo jumps.
1. Stand upright with good posture and engaged abdominal muscles to keep pelvis tucked under body.
2. Use the ankle and foot to jump with minimal bend at the knees.
3. Once in the air pull the toes up towards the shin into a dorsiflexed position so that the foot is in the correct position for the landing.
4. Land on both feet and aim to spend as little time on the ground as possible.
5. Repeat no more than six times, followed by a short break and one more set of six jumps.

A skips.

1. With good posture and upright trunk, bounce lightly on both feet.
2. Start to lift each foot on alternate bounces into a high knee position whilst you bounce on the other foot.
3. Focus on good upright posture and pulling knee into good high knee position with quad parallel to the ground, shin vertical and toes in dorsiflexion.
4. Ensure you keep trunk upright and do not lean backwards.
5. As you become more proficient try to minimise ground contact time on each skip.

A Skips

A skips are among the core running drills but can be difficult to master at first. It can be helpful to slow the drill down to a walk to start to find the rhythm.

Grapevines (overleaf)

Grapevines challenge your coordination through counter-rotation between hips and shoulders (meaning they move in opposite directions).

Grapevines.

1. Face sideways to the direction of travel and keep arms outstretched to the sides throughout.
2. Step sideways with your left foot.
3. Step to the side with your right foot crossing behind your left foot.
4. Step sideways with your left foot again.
5. Step sideways with your right foot crossing in front of your left foot.
6. Return by leading with the opposite foot. To do this, start by facing the same direction but travelling in the opposite direction. Then lead with your right foot stepping sideways before crossing over with your left foot.

3 Strength Training for Masters Runners

If you're too fit for your legs, eventually they will fail.

Sometimes you read a sentence that resonates so strongly that it literally stops you in your tracks, especially if you strip away the technical terms and lay bare the core meaning. In this case the actual sentence was:

> *If the physiological capacity of the body exceeds the biomechanical capacity then continued physiological training without focus on the biomechanical deficiencies will eventually lead to plateau or breakdown.*
>
> Joanne Elphinston, *Stability, Sport & Performance Movement* (2008)

As an elite athlete I thought I did my fair share of strength and conditioning but my focus was always on running more to get faster. The relationship between knocking vital seconds off my PB seemed more closely related to running extra kilometres than strength.

But now I know better. As a Masters runner (and even more so if you are female) strength training is fundamental to keep you running.

The previous chapter introduced the concepts of basic movements and running drills. This chapter builds on those exercises and helps you to progress into strength training. But first let's discuss why strength training is so important for Masters.

Key Issues for Masters Runners

As we get older we experience loss of muscle mass and a decrease in muscular strength partly due to reductions in levels of reproductive hormones. The good news is that focused

> *As I did more running I also picked up a few injuries. I started to see the physio and realised I needed to do other things too (not just running) to make me more robust and prevent injuries. So I started seeing a personal trainer weekly and doing strength work.*
>
> Katherine

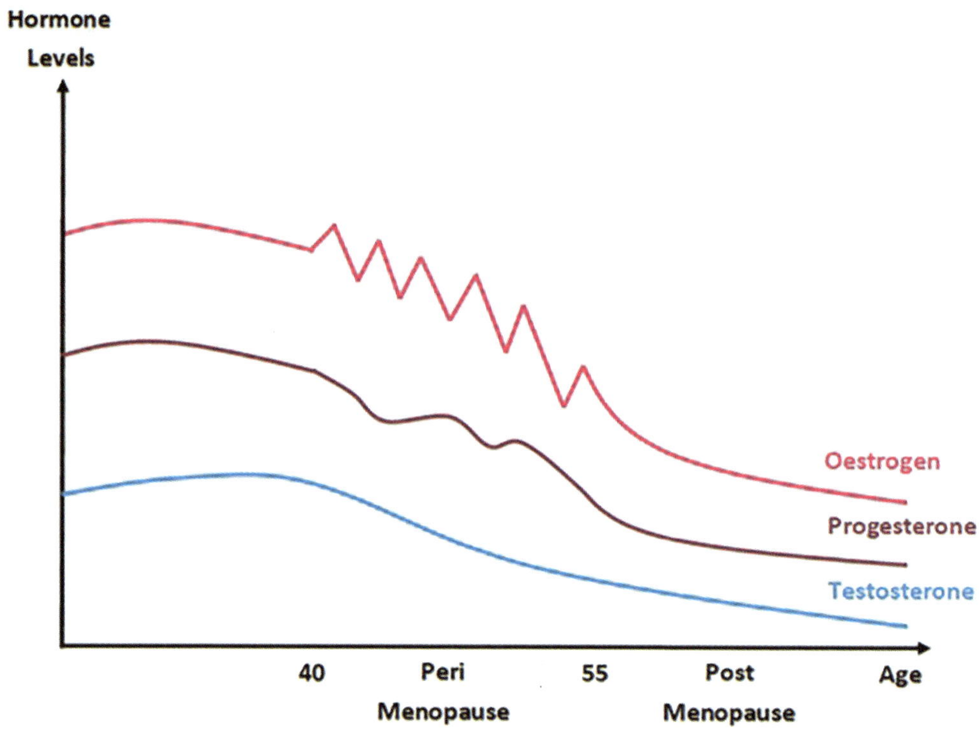

The impact of age on female hormones. The decrease in female reproductive hormones during and post menopause has a significant impact on strength.

strength work with heavier weights helps to both maintain what you have and minimise further age-related loss. Even better for newer runners, the introduction of strength work for relatively untrained individuals provides significant scope to improve muscle mass and strength regardless of age.

In females one of the lesser-known roles of oestrogen is to enhance muscle growth as well as prevent muscle breakdown. Female testosterone levels are significantly lower than males but, as for males, testosterone also plays a key role in muscle growth. Both oestrogen and testosterone drop significantly during perimenopause onwards (usually from late forties to early fifties) and likewise volume of muscle mass and muscle strength starts to dramatically decline in females.

Loss of oestrogen may be partially mediated by Hormone Replacement Therapy (HRT). However, even with HRT the need for strength work to maintain muscle strength remains important. Testosterone is not usually prescribed for females as a standard part of HRT (in the UK) but may be prescribed in exceptional circumstances. However, you should be aware that testosterone is currently a prohibited substance under World Anti-Doping Agency regulations. If you are prescribed testosterone and you wish to compete in races you must familiarise yourself with anti-doping regulations and discuss treatment options with your doctor.

For male runners the decline in testosterone is less dramatic and the loss of strength is more gradual. However, as males move into their sixties the rate of decline increases more steeply and loss of muscle mass and strength becomes more significant. There is currently no standard equivalent to HRT for men. As for females, testosterone is not permitted under World Anti-Doping Agency regulations.

Older people also experience significant declines in bone density over time. This is more significant in females due to the role of oestrogen in bone health. Post-menopausal females may lose up to 2–3 per cent of bone mass per year. For both male and female Masters runners, the decline in bone density significantly increases the risk of stress responses and stress fractures.

To compound the loss of muscle mass, the process of protein synthesis to repair muscle tissue becomes less efficient as we age. For non-runners any weight-bearing activity is helpful. But for runners, because

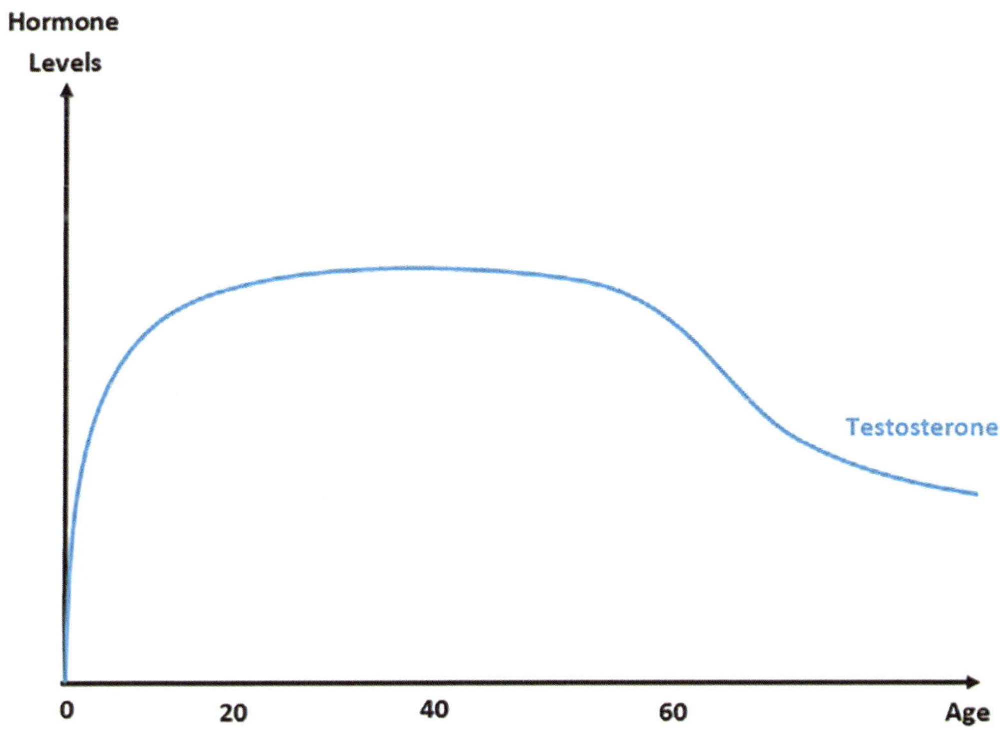

The impact of age on male hormones. The decrease in male reproductive hormones over time has a gradual impact on strength.

the load on your body is greater, there comes a point when running by itself does not provide sufficient training stimulus to maintain the muscle mass and strength required.

Important Advice for Strength Work

Strength workouts don't need to be extensive or complex. But they do need to be regular and consistent to help you maintain your muscle strength. Ideally that means one to two times per week minimum. Any less and you will not get the necessary training stimulus to tackle the significant muscle loss over time.

It's also important to increase your strength work progressively just as you would for running. This means increasing repeats or resistance over time. This does not mean every workout or every week but periodically, subject to your progress.

As a Masters runner I know that time is at a premium. Workouts don't necessarily require going to the gym. However, home workouts will need some weights and specialist equipment to meet the requirements of effective strength training.

Sets of resistance bands are relatively inexpensive and widely available, so these are definitely worth investing in. If you don't have the space or finances for a full squat rack and set of weights, then adjustable dumbbells can be useful to allow you to increase weights as you progress. However, even with just a small selection of weights you can still do an effective strength programme, so don't let lack of equipment hold you back.

Most importantly though, before you get started with heavy weights it is fundamentally important to get good quality, face to face instruction. Effective and safe technique is critical. Poor technique will not only limit the effectiveness of your sessions but more importantly can result in serious injury.

Consider this chapter as a guide to the type of exercises and lifts that should be specifically included in your programme as a Masters runner. But you must ensure you know how to perform each exercise properly before doing so and especially before adding any significant weight.

> *Five or six years ago I was going from one injury to the next because I wasn't doing any strength work. Now I do my routine at least once and mostly twice each week and it's made all the difference.*
>
> John

Key Muscle Groups for Strength Training

Upper body

Endurance runners often neglect the upper body, shoulders and arms as upper body strength is less directly transferable to running. However, it's important for older people to maintain upper body strength for everyday life and to enable you to perform important compound exercises such as squats, dead lifts and press-ups.

Key Terminology for Strength Training for Masters

If you have never done strength training before then the terminology can be unfamiliar and off-putting, so it's helpful to set out some key terms:

Maximum strength: The total amount of force your muscles can generate. Your strength training should include some focus on maximum strength to provide the high level of stimulus required to maintain your muscle strength for as long as possible.

Strength endurance: The amount of force your muscles can continue to repeatedly generate over an extended period of time. Strength endurance is a key focus for endurance runners to enable you to maintain your form over 5k to half marathon.

Power: The amount of force your muscles can generate in the shortest period of time. Power is generally improved by a combination of increased maximum strength and speed of movement. As neuromuscular pathways become less effective and tendon stiffness and elasticity declines as you age it is important to include some power exercises in your training. Power movements for runners include jumps and hops.

Bodyweight: Bodyweight exercises are those that do not use any additional weights or resistance bands. They are good for beginners to develop technique before weight is added. Examples include basic squats or lunges. However, some bodyweight exercises such as press-ups or chin-ups can be very challenging in their own right.

One rep max: The maximum load or weight you can lift in one rep. One rep max tends to be associated with maximum strength training.

Resistance: The load or weight used in the exercise. Usually described in kilograms, but may also be described in terms of percentage of one rep max (*see* above) or occasionally percentage of bodyweight. You should start with lower resistance as you perfect your technique and then aim to work up to heavier resistance as you build up your strength training.

Reps: The number of times you repeat the exercise. In general, the higher the resistance the lower the number of reps performed. Development of maximum strength usually involves sets of three to five reps and strength endurance usually involves five to ten reps. Power exercises and jumps should include no more than five to six exercises or jumps per set.

Set: The number of reps completed before you take a longer break. A workout usually consists of one to three sets.

Recovery: The rest between reps and sets. One common mistake for endurance athletes is to cut the required recovery short because they are unused to neuromuscular fatigue. Neuromuscular fatigue feels very different to the muscular and physiological fatigue usually experienced in running. Hence you feel ready to go again before you are fully physiologically recovered. In general, strength training requires three to five minutes recovery between sets.

Reps in reserve: The number of additional reps you can do before you start to lose your technical form or cannot complete any more reps. Quality over quantity is key for strength training. Reps in reserve is an important measure of how many reps are appropriate for you in each exercise. Most exercises should be performed to one to two reps in reserve.

Trunk

Weakness in the trunk, either abdominal or lower back, can both be responsible for poor posture. As these muscle groups get weaker in older people it's important to build strength in your trunk to enable you to hold your torso upright and absorb the force from running.

Glutes and hamstrings

The glutes play a key role in stabilising the leg during the initial ground contact and preventing excessive strain on the knee from inward and downward collapse.

The hamstrings work to pull the leg back during the running action and bend the knee. They may overwork if glutes are weak or not engaged.

Calf and Achilles tendon

The lower leg absorbs a large proportion of the force during initial ground contact. The calf muscles drive the body upwards and forwards on each step. The Achilles tendon needs to be robust to effectively store the elastic energy required to propel you forwards.

Ankle and Feet

Lack of stability and limited mobility in the ankle are key issues for Masters runners. Focusing on foot and ankle strength enables you to absorb the force of ground contact and maintain stability as you push off.

Bodyweight Exercises

As with running, in strength training you need to build a strong base before you can progress onto harder and heavier workouts. Unlike running, where you can get away with a multitude of sins, good technique is essential from the start.

For all newcomers to strength training, it's advisable to start with bodyweight exercises to learn basic movement patterns before you start to load exercises with weights.

Plank

Planks are an excellent but simple exercise to develop trunk capacity. Front planks work the abdominal muscles and help develop strong upright posture.

Plank.

1. Rest on your elbows with shoulders slightly in front of elbows.
2. Feet should be approximately shoulder width apart.
3. Tighten abdominal muscles and engage glutes to hold body aligned.
4. Keep head aligned with torso and do not allow it to drop downwards.

Side plank.

1. Rest on one elbow with feet on top of each other.
2. Tighten abdominal muscles and engage glutes to hold body aligned.
3. Keep head aligned with torso and do not allow it to drop downwards.

Side Plank

Side planks focus more on the oblique or side muscles and reduce sideways leans and excessive rotation during running.

Press-Ups

Press-ups are an extension from the plank with added focus on development of upper body strength.

Glute Bridge

Glute bridges strengthen the glutes and improve stability around the pelvis. Ideally, they are single leg exercises, but you can start with double legs as you develop your technique.

Hamstring Bridge

Hamstring bridges are similar to glute bridges, except straight legs ensure they engage hamstrings rather than glutes. They can also be single or double leg exercises. Unlike glute bridges these are isometric exercises, which means you hold one position rather than move through a range.

Calf Raises (overleaf)

Calf raises build strength in the calf muscles and Achilles tendon. They can be double leg or single leg. There are two versions: straight legs to strengthen gastrocnemius, or bent knees to strengthen soleus. They can be further adapted to eccentrically load the Achilles tendon. Eccentric loading is

Press-ups.

1. Rest on hands which are pointed forwards, slightly wider than shoulder width apart and aligned with the chest.
2. Brace through abdominal muscles and glutes to hold trunk aligned and not allow hips to sag.
3. Gently lower chest to the floor.
4. Elbows should remain close to the body and not flare outwards.
5. Push up through arms to return to start position.

Glute bridge.

1. Lie on your back with knees bent and feet flat to floor and tuck pelvis underneath body.
2. Lift hips by squeezing glutes whilst keeping shoulders on the ground. Knees should be bent to approximately 90 degrees.
3. For single leg glute bridges straighten one leg outwards and keep it aligned with the weight-bearing leg. For double leg glute bridges keep both feet on floor.
4. Gently lower hips to the ground keeping the other leg outstretched.
5. Squeeze glutes to lift hips again back to start position.

Hamstring bridge.

1. Lie on back with legs outstretched and feet resting on the floor or a low box. Ensure toes are pulled towards shins.
2. Press both heels into the floor or box to lift body from hips, keeping shoulders on the ground.
3. Hold this position for up to 60 seconds.
4. For single leg hamstring bridges, hold one leg above you with knee bent at 90 degrees.

Calf raises.

1. Stand upright with either straight leg (full extension at the hip and knee) or slightly bent at the knee approximately 30–45 degrees.
2. Lift up onto forefoot.
3. Ensure weight is equally distributed between ball of the foot, big toe and outer toes throughout.

Calf raises with heel drop.

1. Stand with forefoot on edge of step and heel overhanging.

2. Ensure weight is equally distributed between ball of foot, big toe and outer toes.

3. Start by lowering heel as low as permitted by ankle mobility.

4. Then push through floor to raise onto forefoot as for calf raise.

when the muscle is lengthened under load rather than shortened or contracted and is significantly more effective for developing strength in tendons.

Pallof press.

1. Stand side onto frame with resistance band looped around it at approximately chest height.
2. Hold resistance band with both hands in fist against the chest.
3. Brace trunk against the force from the band pulling body sideways.
4. Holding this brace position, move hands out from chest to straighten arms and back again.

Low Resistance Exercises

Exercises with resistance bands provide an additional load and challenge the body to work harder to maintain stability and control.

Pallof Press

Pallof presses are trunk and abdominal exercises that develop strength to brace against rotational forces in the trunk when running.

Crab walks.

1. Put resistance band around ankle or knees subject to level of resistance. Band should be under tension when feet are shoulder width apart.
2. Ensure knees turned slightly outwards throughout exercise and do not let knees drift inwards at any point.
3. Squat slightly but not into full squat position. Ensure you achieve squat by moving hips backwards to lower torso rather than bending knees. Knees should not extend forward beyond toes.
4. Keep band on tension throughout.
5. Step sideways in one direction, then back sideways in the other direction, keeping facing forwards throughout.

Crab Walks

These engage your glutes to stabilise legs and knees.

High knee marches.

1. Stand upright with good posture.
2. Put band around both feet.
3. Brace through trunk to maintain upright posture throughout and do not allow torso to lean back.
4. Lift one knee into high knee position (90 degrees at hip, knee and ankle) whilst keeping standing leg straightened.
5. Lower and repeat with opposite knee.

High Knee Marches

High knee marches with a resistance band work hip flexors and stabilising muscles in the trunk.

Foot Inversions

Foot inversions work the tibialis posterior tendon, which supports the ankle and arch of the foot, and prevents it from collapsing on ground contact.

1. Put resistance band around ball of foot and fix to another point on outside of foot.
2. Pull foot inwards against resistance in a gentle movement, hold briefly and slowly move back to starting position.
3. Ensure you only move the foot and keep the shin vertical throughout.

High Resistance Exercises with Weights

The final stage in strength work is to introduce weights. These can be either hand-held weights, such as kettle-bells or dumb-bells, or weights on barbells, subject to equipment available.

Back Squats or Goblet Squats (overleaf)

Squats are one of the fundamental movement patterns. They are a compound exercise that works the whole body including trunk stability, glutes, quads, hip flexors, calf muscles and feet. All runners (regardless of age) should work on how to master a basic squat (as described in Chapter 2). From there you can start to load your squat.

Back squats enable you to achieve the heaviest loads and therefore maximise the development of strength. However, as you develop your technique and strength, or in the absence of a barbell and squat rack, you can start with goblet squats, in which the weight is held by both hands in front of the chest.

Back squats and goblet squats.

1. Feet should be positioned slightly wider than shoulder width with toes turned slightly outwards.
2. Weight should be maintained through the whole foot (not tipping onto toes or heels) and feet should remain flat on the floor throughout.
3. Lower body into squat position by pushing hips backwards.
4. Knees should remain aligned with toes and not drift inwards.
5. Trunk should remain neutral.
6. Lower until thighs parallel with the ground or trunk cannot remain relatively upright or feet cannot remain flat.

Dead lifts.
1. Stand with feet shoulder width apart.
2. Engage abdominal muscles to brace through the trunk and hinge at the waist, move upper body downwards to grasp the bar.
3. Keep arms straightened throughout.
4. Push through feet, squeeze glutes and bring hips forwards to lift the bar from the floor, ensuring that it remains in contact with shins and quads as it is raised.

Dead Lifts

Dead lifts involve lifting weights from the floor and work to strengthen hamstrings and glutes. Dead lifts require the ability to hinge effectively at the hips and develop good hip mobility.

Single Leg Romanian Dead Lifts (RDLs) (overleaf)

Romanian dead lifts differ from dead lifts in that the weight is not raised and lowered from the floor. They can lessen the load on knees if required. Romanian dead lifts may be double leg or single leg. It can be useful to start with double leg to develop technique before progressing on to single leg to address any imbalances between leg strength.

Single leg Romanian dead lifts.

1. Hold weights in both hands and keep arms straightened throughout.

2. Engage abdominal muscles and hinge at the waist.

3. Keep hips level and facing forwards, and the rear leg aligned with trunk as it lifts.

Bulgarian squats.

1. Raise one leg by putting foot on chair behind.
2. Keep pelvis neutral and lower into squat, ensuring you move hips backwards into good squat position.
3. Ensure you keep knee aligned with foot and do not allow it to fall inwards at any point.
4. Push up from the floor and keep majority of weight on front foot.

Bulgarian Squats

These target the glutes and lower leg, similar to back squats, but as single leg exercises they help to address imbalances in leg strength.

Weighted Calf Raises

Double leg calf raises can be performed with a barbell or holding a weight to the chest. Single leg calf raises enable you to focus on individual leg strength and can be performed with a barbell or holding a weight in one hand on the weight-bearing side. As before, calf raises can be bent leg or straight leg and may also include a heel drop to target the Achilles tendon.

Weighted calf raises.

Jumps

Jumps focus on the development of power, tendon stiffness and elasticity as well as improving the effectiveness of neural muscular pathways and the recruitment of muscle fibres. All these qualities decline significantly with age if they are not addressed via regular strength workouts.

Drop Jumps

Drop jumps are plyometric exercises that aim to improve elasticity and reactivity off the ground. The aim is to step off a low box then rebound as quickly as possible upwards so that you spend as little time in ground contact as you can. It's important to ensure your foot is dorsiflexed (toe up) as you step off and land so that you can engage the Achilles tendon in the stretch shortening cycle.

Drop jumps

1. Stand on box.
2. Lift one foot forward off side of box.
3. Drop and land on both feet ensuring you land on flat foot.
4. Once you have mastered the technique for drop jumps add a rebound jump.
5. As above, but as soon as you land jump upwards as high as possible by swinging arms back and up and bending knees.

Countermovement jumps
1. Start with feet shoulder width apart and hands on hips.
2. Lower into squat position then push up from the floor to jump upwards, keeping hands on hips and focusing on moving with speed throughout both movements.
3. Land evenly on both feet.
4. Aim for no more than five or six jumps.

Countermovement Jumps

Countermovement jumps are great to develop power. Running is a dynamic movement, so power is essential even for endurance runners.

Pogos

Pogos were described as part of running drills but they are in fact plyometric exercises.

1. Stand upright with good posture and engaged trunk muscles.
2. Use the ankle and foot to jump with minimal bend at the knees.
3. Once in the air, pull the toes up towards the shin into a dorsiflexed position so that the foot is in the correct position for the landing.
4. Land on both feet and aim to spend as little time on the ground as possible.
5. Repeat no more than six times, followed by a short break and one more set of six jumps.

Strength Training Plans

As a Masters runners your aim is to improve strength and strength endurance. For strength development, you should gradually work towards heavier weights with which you can manage two or three reps before you lose form.

For strength endurance you should aim for medium to heavy weights with six to eight reps. However, for any individual exercise always be guided by the number of reps you can perform before you are unable to maintain the correct form and stop at this point. As you improve strength you should aim to add progression by adding weight rather than additional reps.

Included here are two workout plans per week for each level.

Introduction to Strength Workout 1	
Exercise (2–3 sets each exercise)	**Reps/Duration**
Bodyweight squats	10–20 reps
Plank	20sec to 2min
Hamstring bridge (double leg)	20sec to 2min
Single leg calf raises (straight leg on step with heel drop)	8–20 reps per leg
Crab walks with resistance band	3 × 10 steps in each direction
Foot inversions with resistance band	5–20 reps each foot

Introduction to Strength Workout 2	
Exercise (2–3 sets each exercise)	**Reps**
Pogo jumps	3–6 jumps
Glute bridges (single leg)	10–20 per leg
Double leg calf raises with bent knee	8–20
High knee marches with resistance band	8–20 per leg
Pallof press	8–20 each side

Intermediate Strength Workout 1	
Exercise (2–3 sets each exercise)	**Reps**
Countermovement jumps	3–5 jumps
Squats with medium resistance	10–15 reps
Single leg Romanian dead lift with medium resistance	8–15 reps per leg
Single leg calf raises with weight	8–15 reps each leg
Plank	20sec to 2min
Foot inversions with resistance band	5–20 reps per foot

Intermediate Strength Workout 2	
Exercise (2–3 sets each exercise)	**Reps/Duration**
Pogo jumps	3–5 jumps
Press-ups	5–20
Bulgarian squats with medium resistance	10–15 reps per leg
Hamstring bridge with medium resistance	20sec to 20min
Double leg calf raises with weight	8–15 reps

Advanced Strength Workout 1	
Exercise (2–3 sets each exercise)	**Reps/Duration**
Drop jumps	3–5 jumps
Squats with heavy resistance (back squat or goblet squat)	6–8 reps
Single leg RDLs with heavy resistance	6–8 reps each leg
Straight leg single leg calf raises with heavy resistance	10–12 reps each leg
Plank	Up to 60sec

Advanced Strength Workout 2	
Exercise (2–3 sets each exercise)	**Reps**
Pogo jumps	5 jumps
Dead lifts with heavy resistance	6–8 reps
Bulgarian split squats with heavy resistance	6–8 reps
Double leg calf raises with heavy resistance	10–12 reps
Pallof press	8–10 reps

4 Warm-Up and Cool-Down

I'll just warm up as I go along.

How many times have you heard runners say this? An effective warm-up is important for athletes of all ages but even more so as we get older. The warm-up is often seen as the optional part of the workout if you are short of time, whereas a good quality warm-up is actually one of the best examples of time-saving multitasking in running.

Skipping the warm-up means you compromise the potential training benefits from the first part of your run as your aerobic energy system is not fully operational and the neuromuscular pathways to your muscles are not fully activated. A good quality warm-up does more than just get you ready to run. It also adds an important additional volume of easy running onto your weekly total. Warm-up exercises and running drills double up as important conditioning and mobility workouts for running technique and address some of the common issues that affect performance and longevity in running for Masters. Lastly, a familiar and well-rehearsed warm-up routine helps you set aside stress from your daily life and puts you in the right mindset to perform, whether it's at training or races.

How to Warm Up

An effective warm-up should have four key components, which together comprise the acronym RAMP:

- Raise
- Activation
- Mobilisation
- Potentiation

In practice there is considerable overlap between these components and their associated activities.

My days of turning up, jumping out of the car and running are over. It doesn't work. I break myself and it's so uncomfortable to run if I don't warm up properly

John

Raise

This is the part of the warm-up with which you are probably most familiar. It traditionally comprises continuous easy running, which serves to raise the heart rate and increase blood flow around the body. Along with the increased rate of breathing, this improves the supply and rate of oxygen usage and enables you to create more energy through the aerobic energy system. In general, the aerobic energy system takes between ten to twenty minutes to operate at its full capacity to generate maximum energy. This means to be most effective the Raise component should include ten to fifteen minutes of jogging plus running drills and plyometric exercises.

Activation

This component seeks to activate the neuromuscular connections between the brain and the key groups of muscles used to run. Activation exercises start with simple bodyweight movements followed by exercises with resistance bands to fully engage the muscles. Typical exercises might include foot drills, high knee walks or marches, lunges and squats.

Mobilisation

Mobilisation increases the range of movement of key muscles through more vigorous and dynamic exercises. Key exercises might include leg swings, hamstring sweeps, hurdle mobility drills and running drills such as high knees, A skips, B skips and dribbles.

Potentiation

Potentiation is the final stage of an effective warm-up and the one most often missed (or misunderstood) by endurance runners.

Potentiation is when you perform short bursts of higher intensity activity in order to stimulate the nervous system and improve the strength, power or efficiency of subsequent activity. Ideally the potentiation activity should be relatively brief (in comparison to the duration of the activity to follow) and should not generate any lasting fatigue.

For faster intervals sessions (5k pace or faster), potentiation might comprise progressive or fast 200 to 300 metres strides. For 5k to half marathon races or threshold sessions it might involve short blocks (one to three minutes) of threshold running before being followed by some shorter, faster strides.

You should aim to have between three to five minutes between your final potentiation exercise and the start of the race or workout to allow any fatigue to dissipate but still gain maximum benefit from the stimulus.

How Long is the Warm-Up?

Your warm-up should be between 20 to 60 minutes. In general, the length of the warm-up should be relative to the intensity of effort and the importance of the workout or race to follow.

However, you also have to be pragmatic and you may be constrained by your time available. Not many of us have the time to engage in a fully comprehensive 60-minute warm-up before every run. In general, I suggest these guidelines:

- For faster paced intervals (5k pace or faster) or key races you should aim to warm up for 30–60 minutes in order to be fully warmed up and ready to run fast from the start. Your warm-up should include all the four components of an effective warm-up.
- For lower intensity workouts, such as fartleks or progression runs, you can shorten your warm-up to 20 minutes as you are aiming to start your session at a lower level of intensity, which requires less warm-up.
- For easy runs you can potentially shorten your warm-up to 5–10 minutes and focus more on activation and mobilisation.

Common Problems with Warm-Ups

Does it take a significant period of time at the start of your run or intervals session for your breathing to settle down?
This suggests you need to spend longer on the raise component of your warm-up or add some potentiation. Increase the pace or duration of your easy jogging and add some more dynamic drills. Finish with a potentiation activity to ensure your aerobic energy system is operating at full capacity before you start the race or intervals session.
Do you struggle to move smoothly when you start running or feel like you are 'hobbling' along for the first few minutes?
Start your warm-up with some activation and mobilisation exercises to improve your range of movement and increase neuromuscular engagement of muscles before you start running.
Do you struggle to find the right pace at the start of your intervals or races?
Focus on potentiation at the end of your warm-up by adding a short threshold block or some faster-paced strides at your intended race pace or pace for your intervals. This helps you to be ready to perform at the required intensity from the start.
Do you feel tired after your warm-up when you start your session?
You may need to reduce the volume or intensity of your warm-up or allow a greater period of recovery between the potentiation activity and the start of your session or race.

Cool-Down

The aim of the cool-down is to return your mind and body to its pre-exercise state. Traditionally the cool-down comprises some easy jogging.

Contrary to common belief, there is limited conclusive evidence that cool-downs have major impact on recovery, reduction in blood lactate levels or muscle soreness. However, many runners feel that a cool-down jog makes them feel better after harder workouts or races.

The psychological benefits of the cool-down are equally important. It allows time for relaxed social interaction, which is equally if not more valuable to recovery than other recovery methods that are also potentially more expensive, such as massage therapy, hydrotherapy, sauna or compression.

Easy jogging

In general, the cool-down should comprise five to fifteen minutes of relaxed, easy jogging. Unlike the warm-up, there is

Warm-Up Plans

Full warm-up (30–60min)
Suitable for races or intervals sessions.

Exercise	Number of reps/time/ distances	Component of warm-up
Easy to moderate pace jogging	10–20 mins	Raise
Toe taps	3 × 20m	Activation and mobilisation
Heel walks	3 × 20m	Activation and mobilisation
Heel to toe foot rolls	3 × 20m	Activation and mobilisation
Crab walks	2 × 10 steps each direction	Activation
Bodyweight squats	8–10	Activation
Reverse lunge to high knee	6–8 each leg	Activation and mobilisation
Hamstring sweeps	10 each leg	Mobilisation
High knee walk	3 × 20m	Mobilisation
High knee drills	3 × 20m	Raise and mobilisation
Heel kicks	3 × 20m	Raise and mobilisation
Grapevines	2 × 20m each direction	Raise and mobilisation
Pogos	3 × 5 jumps	Raise and mobilisation
Dribbles	3 × 20m	Raise and mobilisation
Scissor kicks	3 × 20m	Raise and mobilisation
A drills	3 × 20m	Raise and mobilisation
EITHER Threshold potentiation (threshold, 10k to half marathon pace intervals session or race)	3 mins easy threshold run 1 min recovery 3 × 20 secs progressive paced strides	Raise and potentiation
OR		
Threshold & 5k potentiation (threshold, VO_2 max or 5k to 10k pace session or race)	1 min threshold pace 1 min recovery 2 × 30sec fast strides	Raise and potentiation
OR		
5k & VO_2 max potentiation (5k, VO_2 max or faster session or race)	3 × 30–40sec progressive paced strides	Raise and potentiation

Medium Warm-Up (20min)

Suitable for mid intensity sessions, such as fartleks or threshold runs, or when short of time.

Exercise	Number of reps/time/ distances	Component of warm-up
Easy to moderate pace jogging	10–15min	Raise
Toe taps	1 × 20m	Activation and mobilisation
Heel walks	1 × 20m	Activation and mobilisation
Bodyweight squats	5–6	Activation
Reverse lunge to high knee	3–5 each leg	Activation and mobilisation
Hamstring sweeps	10 each leg	Mobilisation
High knee drills	2 × 20m	Raise and mobilisation
Heel kicks	2 × 20m	Raise and mobilisation
Grapevines	2 × 20m each direction	Raise and mobilisation
Dribbles	2 × 20m	Raise and mobilisation
A drills	2 × 20m	Raise and mobilisation
EITHER		
Threshold & 5k potentiation (threshold, VO_2 max or 5k to 10k pace session or race)	1 min threshold pace 1min recovery 2 × 30–40sec fast strides	Raise and potentiation
OR		
5k & VO_2 max potentiation (5k, VO_2 max or faster session or race)	3 × 30–40sec progressive paced strides	Raise and potentiation

Quick Warm-Up (10min)

Suitable for easy runs or when you are very short of time. Note this warm-up will not be effective to provide full benefits of warm-up before faster paced training or races.

Exercise	Number of reps/time/ distances	Component of warm-up
Easy to moderate pace jogging (optional on easy runs)	5 mins (optional)	Raise
Toe taps	10 steps	Activation and mobilisation
Heel walks	10 steps	Activation and mobilisation
Bodyweight squats	3	Activation and mobilisation
Reverse lunge to high knee	2 each leg	Activation and mobilisation
Hamstring sweeps	3 each leg	Mobilisation
Pogos	2 × 5 jumps	Raise and mobilisation
Potentiation strides	2 × 30 secs progressive paced strides	Raise and potentiation

Adjustments to Warm-Up for Weather

Warm weather

Although you may feel warm before you start, you still need to ensure that your aerobic energy system is fully operational before your session or race. If it's exceptionally warm you may wish to remove additional clothing before you start the warm-up, reduce the jogging component and swap to drills that you may be able to do in shade, if available. Ensure you remain hydrated by sipping water and cool yourself by dousing your head with water.

Cold or wet weather

Ensure you remain warm and dry by keeping on additional layers and waterproof layers for as long as possible during your warm-up. If it's cold you may wish to extend the jogging part of your warm-up by five minutes and reduce the activation and mobilisation exercises as these are less active, to avoid getting colder and wetter unless there is an indoor space available.

more debate about the training benefits of additional easy running in the cool-down.

If you are already fatigued from the session then an extended cool-down may only serve to add extra fatigue and increase the risk of injury in return for very limited additional training benefits. There is also some evidence that if your session focused on anaerobic adaptations then these may be partially inhibited by the additional aerobic demands from the extended cool-down.

In general, my advice would be to avoid adding extra kilometres onto your cool-down. If you want to add extra weekly volume, then ideally seek to put this elsewhere into your training.

Cool-Down Stretches

Whilst it is generally accepted that static stretching has limited value in your warm-up, it is also generally accepted that it may be beneficial as part of the cool-down.

To be effective, stretches should be held for a minimum of 30 to 60 seconds. You should ensure you are stable and well balanced and keep the muscles fully relaxed. Do not stretch beyond what is comfortable. Stop if you feel any soreness or pain.

Key Stretches for Cool-Down

Lower back.

1. Lie on your side with the upper knee bent over and gently resting on the floor.
2. Use the opposite hand to hold your knee in this position.
3. Rotate your upper body and allow shoulders to lie as flat as possible on the floor with your arm outstretched and head turned to the side.

Hip flexor lunge (hip flexors).

1. Lower into lunge position and push hips forwards.
2. Ensure that your abdominal muscles are engaged and pelvis does not move to maximise hip flexor stretch.
3. You can increase the range of the stretch by raising up your arm.

Child's pose (lower back).

1. Kneel on the ground sitting back on your heels.
2. Bend your upper body over and stretch forwards with arms.

Knee to chest (glutes and lower back).

1. Lie on back.
2. Pull knee to chest and hold.

Standing hamstring.

1. Stand with one leg gently outstretched forwards and heel gently resting on the ground.
2. Sit back onto hips and hinge upper body over to try to put torso as close to your upper leg as possible.
3. Rest hands gently on knees for stability.

Standing quad.

1. Stand and pull one knee behind you to stretch quad.
2. Hold on to wall for balance if needed.

Straight leg calf stretch.

1. Stand facing the wall with both feet facing forwards and one foot in front of the other.
2. Ensure both feet are aligned and facing forwards, not turned outwards or inwards.
3. Keep the back leg straight and foot flat to the floor.
4. Lean forwards until you feel the stretch in your calf.

Bent knee calf stretch

1. As for straight leg calf stretch, but bring rear foot closer to front foot.
2. Bend knee to focus stretch on soleus and Achilles tendon.

5 Basic Nutrition for Masters Runners

These days we are bombarded by often contradictory messages about nutrition, along with an array of glitzy marketing promising to transform our bodies and our performance with their products. This chapter aims to provide some basic, robust, evidence-backed practical advice to guide you through this maze.

In very simple terms the best way to maximise your performance through nutrition is to eat enough to fuel your running. And that means energy-rich carbohydrates: bread, pasta and rice.

For older runners this regular carbohydrate intake should be supported by regular protein throughout the day to promote muscle repair and maintenance. Dairy milk and eggs are two of the most effective ways to consume all of the essential proteins you need.

Why is Nutrition Important for Masters Runners

Energy comes from the food that we eat. Our overall energy needs are the energy required for exercise and daily activity along with the energy required for essential physiological processes such as breathing, heart function, body temperature, digestion and reproductive functions.

Energy availability is what is left after the energy for the essential physiological processes has been deducted. If energy intake (how much we eat) is too little or energy demands from exercise are too great, then we will not have sufficient energy availability and performance and health will start to suffer.

Losing weight was important to me but I am also always quite conscious of the level of energy that needs to be bagged before my runs. So I don't compromise on getting the energy I need which means a decent breakfast. That means its very rare that I run poorly because there's not enough fuel.

Hervé

Low energy availability is undesirable in all runners, but in Masters it further exacerbates the challenges of training whilst ageing, such as reduced muscle mass, less effective muscle repair, lower metabolism, suppressed hormone levels and increased risk of illness and injury. Contrary to popular misconception, energy availability is an important issue for male and female runners.

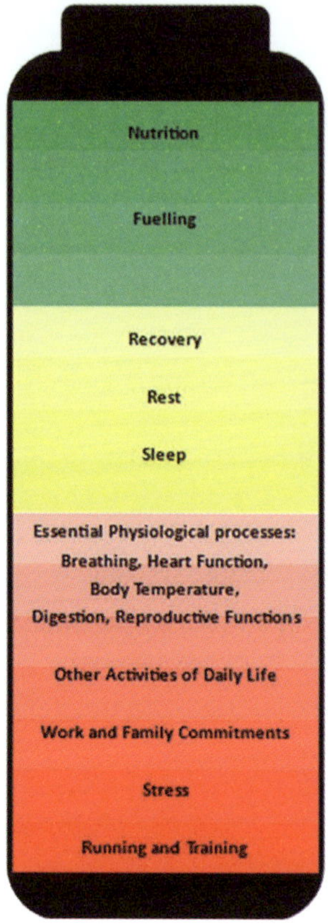

Key factors in energy availability.

Key Nutrition for Masters Runners

Food First

As you might have already grasped, this nutrition advice starts with the key principle known as the 'food first' approach. You should ideally seek to meet all your dietary needs through food before looking to processed and engineered supplements. Whilst some sports nutrition products may be backed by some evidence, the majority cannot fully replicate the range of macro and micronutrients found in real food.

Carbohydrate

Carbohydrates seem to have acquired an unfairly bad reputation as responsible for weight gain and bloating in older age. In fact, carbohydrate is the most important source of energy for runners. It is highly efficient and provides energy more effectively than fat or protein. Carbohydrate is stored in the muscles and liver as glycogen and its purpose is to fuel physical activity alongside important brain function and regulation of how you feel.

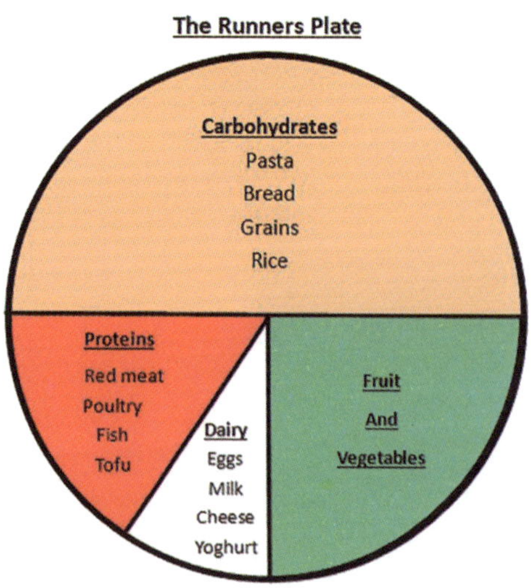

Essential nutrition for Masters runners.

Regular carbohydrates throughout the day are very important for Masters runners due to changes in metabolism that reduce energy efficiency as well as reduced muscle mass, which means the body can store less glycogen.

Timing is key and runners should aim to eat a carbohydrate snack approximately one to four hours before exercise. Glycogen stores should then be replenished with further regular intake after exercise.

Good pre-exercise snacks include:

- Banana
- Dried apricots or raisins
- Cereal bar or flapjack
- Toast with jam or honey
- Porridge
- Cereal with milk

Most main meals should ideally be made up of one-third to one-half carbohydrate such as pasta, bread or rice foods. Snacks and main meals should focus on 'energy dense' foods as described.

One common pitfall to avoid is to fill up on what might be generally considered to be 'healthy foods' such as leaves, vegetables and soft fruits, but which do not contain sufficient carbohydrate to meet your energy needs as a runner.

Protein

Protein synthesis is the biological process by which the body turns protein from food into muscle tissue to build and repair muscle in response to training. Protein synthesis becomes less efficient with age and it is even more important for Masters runners to include sufficient protein in their diet.

The timing of protein intake is critical. Protein synthesis is more effective when protein is consumed within a short period after exercise. Dairy milk (semi or skimmed milk) is generally considered to be one of the most effective post-exercise forms of nutrition as it contains the ideal quantity of both carbohydrate and protein, as well as offering very effective rehydration.

On top of this, protein should also be consumed regularly throughout the day rather than via two or three main meals to promote more efficient muscle growth and repair. There is also some suggestion that Masters runners may also benefit from consuming protein at night before sleep. Your bedtime drink of hot chocolate might be more important than you think.

The best sources of protein for muscle repair are dairy milk or eggs as these contain all of the essential amino acids. Meat, poultry and fish and some plant-based foods including quinoa and tofu are also good sources of complete proteins.

Other good post-exercise protein snacks include:

- Chocolate milk
- Scrambled egg on toast
- Cheese or tuna sandwich
- Baked beans on toast
- Pasta and chicken

Iron

Good iron levels are fundamental for Masters runners as it is essential to form haemoglobin, which transports oxygen in the blood from the lungs to the muscles. Iron deficiency means less oxygen reaches the muscles and less energy can be created. This reduces VO_2 max and significantly reduces endurance. Common symptoms of low iron include increased fatigue, breathlessness, pale skin, dark circles around the eyes and poor performance in running.

Endurance runners should generally aim to have iron levels at the higher end of the normal range because iron is so important. What's more, the demand for iron in runners may be greater due to the increased breakdown of red blood cells from repeated foot strike.

Female runners may be more at risk of iron deficiency due to blood loss during menstruation. Vegan or vegetarian diets may lack iron without careful consideration to ensure sufficient intake. Restricted diets either as part of a weight loss programme or low energy availability also increase the risk of low iron intake.

Good sources of iron include:

- Liver
- Beef
- Eggs
- Dried apricots
- Cashew nuts
- Spinach
- Broccoli
- Red lentils
- Pumpkin seeds

Note that it is not advisable to take iron supplements without a blood test to confirm low iron as they may have harmful side effects.

Calcium

Bone density and calcium uptake reduces with age in both genders, but loss of bone density is much more pronounced in females post menopause. Calcium plays an important role in muscle contractions as well as bone remodelling, so is an important nutrient for Masters runners on several fronts.

Dairy milk is the best source of calcium available but other sources include:

- Cheese
- Yoghurt
- Beans and lentils
- Sardines
- Kale and okra

Relative Energy Deficit in Sport (REDS)

Relative Energy Deficit in Sport or REDS has been recognised as a serious problem, which can affect any runner whether male or female, young or old. REDS arises when energy intake is not sufficient to meet energy demands. In these circumstances the body prioritises the immediate demand for energy to fuel exercise and starts to suppress other important biological functions.

Early signs of REDS include increased fatigue and repeated illness or injury as the immune system starts to become suppressed and muscle repair becomes less efficient. If the energy imbalance continues then the reproductive system shuts down and testosterone and oestrogen levels drop. Bone health starts to be compromised and the risk of stress fractures increases dramatically. This is particularly harmful to Masters runners as it accelerates normal loss of bone density with age.

In female Masters runners the key symptom of loss of menstrual cycle may often be overlooked as it is incorrectly associated with perimenopause.

Key signs of REDS include:

- Feeling run down or tired, which affects daily life
- Increased irritability
- Loss of appetite
- Series of minor illnesses
- Poor sleep
- Persistent aches or pains in muscles or tendons
- Bone stress injuries
- Training starts to become an obsession and it's hard to miss days or step back
- Interruptions to menstrual cycle (female athletes who are not perimenopause or post-menopause)
- Changes to usual pattern of erections (male athletes)

REDS may arise from intentional or unintentional underfuelling (not eating enough to meet energy demands).

Unintentional underfuelling often happens when active individuals fail to realise how much energy is required either just for their sport or through the additional energy demands of higher than average levels of other day-to-day activities. These might include lots of walking or cycling as part of daily life or physically active jobs. Unintentional underfuelling should be relatively easy to resolve with increased daily food intake and potentially some reduction in daily activity.

Intentional underfuelling is more complicated and usually requires professional support from a specialist dietician, nutritionist and psychologist. Signs of intentional underfuelling might include restricting food intake or excluding certain food groups for no valid reasons. It might also include overtraining or continuing to run when rest has been advised, especially if injured or ill.

Whether intentional or not, REDS can have serious, long-term health consequences for Masters runners and will always impact performance: it is a condition that must be addressed.

Impact of Menstrual Cycle and Menopause on Nutrition

Hormone levels change greatly through the menstrual cycle. As progesterone levels rise in the second half of the menstrual cycle, appetite often increases and some women experience cravings as blood sugars fluctuate.

In the luteal and pre-menstrual phase (before your period starts) many runners feel bloated and sluggish in training. During this phase the metabolic rate may increase and the body has to work harder.

Female runners who experience heavy periods may be at higher risk of low iron and should seek medical advice if they start to recognise the symptoms.

During perimenopause, hormone levels may fluctuate even more and some female runners experience an increase in these pre-menstrual symptoms as well as increased frequency of menstruation and heavier blood flow during periods.

Decisions about how to control reproduction are deeply personal and individual. Some female runners find that hormonal contraception and HRT help manage unwanted symptoms that otherwise impact on their running. However, it's important to be aware that hormonal contraception, and to some extent HRT, affect the natural menstrual cycle. This means it cannot be used as the sole marker of good energy availability.

Nutritional Ergogenic Aids to Performance

Nutritional ergogenic aids are nutritional supplements or substances that are specifically consumed to enhance performance. Slick marketing will have you believe that there is a host of products that will make you run faster. For most there is no good evidence. However, there are a limited number of nutritional products that have some (albeit limited) impact on performance.

The key point here, however, is that the best way to improve performance through nutrition is to ensure that you have maximum glycogen available. This means focusing on sufficient carbohydrate intake first. Any other ergogenic aids should supplement and complement your diet.

You must also ensure that you only purchase nutritional ergogenic supplements from reputable manufacturers who batch-test their products under the 'Informed Sport' badge to ensure they are not contaminated with banned substances in contravention of the anti-doping regulations.

Caffeine

The role of caffeine has been studied extensively. It is generally considered that it has the biggest effect on the central nervous system and it works to lower perception of effort. This enables runners to sustain the same pace for longer or to run faster for apparently less effort.

It may benefit runners in a range of distances including 5k to half marathon. Ideally runners should seek to have caffeine approximately 60 minutes prior to performance. Caffeine is widely available in coffee and other forms such as processed energy products.

Nitrates

Nitrates are found in leafy greens and root vegetables and are most commonly consumed in beetroot and beetroot-based products. Nitrates improve the function of mitochondria and improve performance by

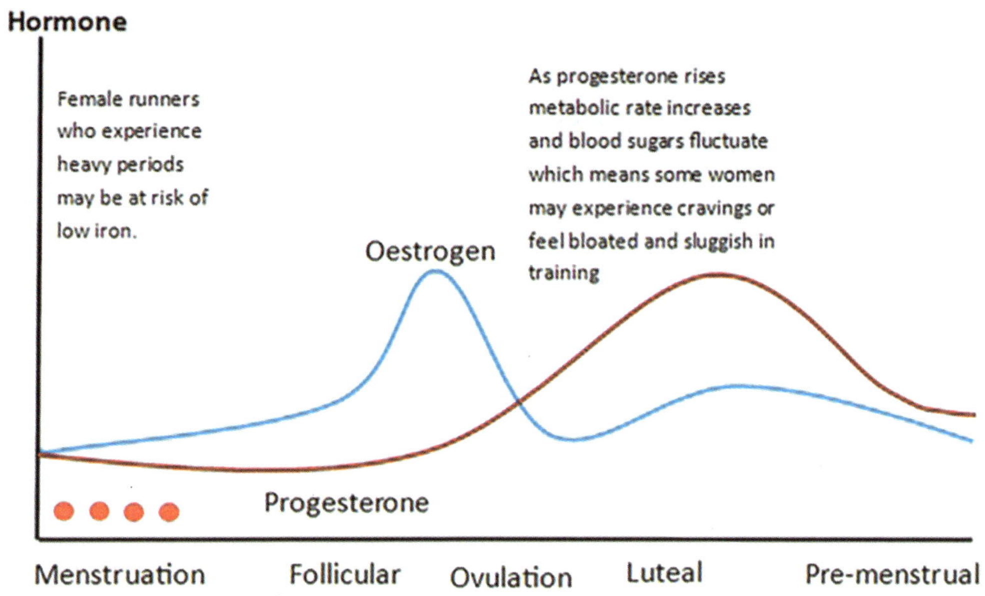

Different stages of the menstrual cycle may have an impact on nutrition.

decreasing the amount of oxygen required to run at threshold pace or slower, which benefits most runners competing in 5k to half marathon.

The most effective quantity and timing for nitrates is still subject to debate. Benefits have been identified from both taking nitrates on the day of the race as well as over the preceding two weeks. There does not appear to be any greater benefits for taking higher doses and these can be associated with unwanted side effects and gastrointestinal issues.

Sodium Bicarbonate

The performance-enhancing properties of sodium bicarbonate have been known about for some time, but until recently they were hard to utilise because they were outweighed by unpleasant and detrimental side effects such as severe gastrointestinal distress and diarrhoea. Recent developments have enabled sodium bicarbonate to be tolerated much better in specially processed products. However, many runners still find it causes bloating, burping and stomach issues.

Sodium bicarbonate works by increasing the alkaline levels in the body, which mitigates the build-up of acidic hydrogen ions, which are waste products from the anaerobic energy system. It delays the onset of muscle fatigue and enables runners to run faster for longer before they are forced to slow down.

Sodium bicarbonate has the biggest impact on performance in middle distance (800m and 1500m) and other events lasting less than ten minutes that are run at higher intensities. For 5k events and longer, the build-up of hydrogen ions is more limited and the impact of sodium bicarbonate on performance is likewise less effective.

Beta Alanine

Beta alanine has a muscle and fatigue buffering effect similar to that of sodium bicarbonate, which enables runners to run faster for longer. But unlike sodium bicarbonate, it needs to be consumed over an extended period of weeks prior to the event.

Beta alanine is found naturally in fish and meat such as chicken, beef and pork. Similar to sodium bicarbonate, its impact on events over ten minutes is more limited.

Creatine

Creatine is a protein that is stored in the muscles and fuels high-intensity activity such as sprinting, or strength work with heavy weights. It is found naturally in meat or fish. As a supplement it is usually taken in powder form and is more beneficial when taken post-exercise. The positive effects of creatine are very well researched. In general it increases muscle mass and improves performance in very high intensity activities, but, there is less evidence of its direct benefit in aerobic activities such as 5k, 10k or half marathon.

For older runners, its positive impact on muscle growth may help maintain muscle mass for longer alongside some evidence of its positive impact on cognitive function. However, its side effects include weight gain due to the increase in muscle mass and increase in water retention in the muscles along with bloating and gastrointestinal issues.

Pre and post run nutrition and refuelling is essential to maximise your performance and recovery. Bananas are one example of an excellent source of carbohydrate.

PART II

HOW TO TRAIN

No human is limited.

Eliud Kipchoge, Olympic gold medallist and marathon world record holder

6 Key Concepts in Endurance and How Training Works

Some runners just like to be told what to do. But from experience the best runners are those who understand a little bit about *how* training works. These runners can then start to make their own decisions about what is best for them as and when they need and become even better runners.

Energy Systems

Let's begin with energy systems. Our metabolic energy systems involve complex biochemistry and physiology. In very simplistic terms these energy systems work by converting the chemical energy of food that we eat into energy for muscle contractions, which then creates movement. We have three metabolic energy systems:

- Aerobic
- Anaerobic or lactate (also known as glycolysis)
- ATP (also known as ATP-CP or creatine phosphate)

We often artificially see these three energy systems as separate and distinct and working in isolation from each other. In fact all three energy systems work together. The contribution of each energy system varies subject to the type, duration and intensity of exercise undertaken and the level of each individual's fitness. So whilst specific training sessions may encourage greater adaptation in one energy system over another, no one run or session exclusively targets or uses just one energy system.

> *Working with a coach has brought me better understanding of how everything is connected whether it's about muscles and tightness, training or tiredness. I have got to know myself a lot better. It has helped me to learn how to decide whether I need to change something, or have an extra rest day or can push on.*
>
> Hervé

ENERGY SYSTEMS

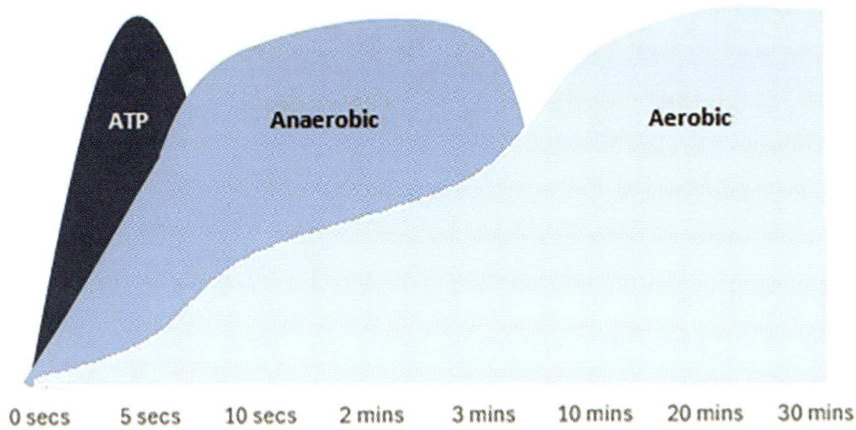

The contribution of each energy system varies subject to type, duration and intensity of exercise.

Aerobic

The aerobic energy system contributes most to 5k to half marathon. This energy system uses oxygen to turn glycogen and fats into energy. It relies on the heart and lungs to transport oxygen around the body as effectively as possible.

However, it takes a significant period of time (usually between ten to twenty minutes) for the aerobic system to reach the point when it operates at its full capacity and generates maximum energy. During this period our other systems contribute a greater proportion of energy usage as we run.

At low to moderate intensity of exercise, which equates to easy pace running for most of us, the aerobic energy system is highly efficient and can produce large quantities of energy over an extended period of time. At this intensity it is also highly resistant to fatigue. However, the maximum rate of energy production is relatively slow.

As intensity of exercise increases when you run faster, the rate of demand and overall demand for energy also increases. Unfortunately, the aerobic energy system cannot create enough energy quickly enough to continue to fully meet these demands. As a result, the anaerobic energy system starts to contribute more of the energy instead. This point is called the lactate threshold or lactate turning point.

The aerobic system is predominantly developed by easy runs over an extended duration (minimum approximately 20 minutes and beyond). As fitness develops the aerobic system is further developed by adding intervals.

Anaerobic (Also Known as Lactate System or Glycolysis)

Whilst the aerobic energy system is the major source of energy in 5k to half marathon, the anaerobic system makes an important contribution. For most runners, 5k is above the lactate turning point where energy production starts to shift towards the anaerobic system.

Even within 10k and half marathon there will be a significant contribution from anaerobic energy, especially at the start and potentially throughout if there are changes in pace or during the final finishing burst.

The anaerobic energy system creates energy from glycogen stored in the muscles through the process of glycolysis. Unlike the aerobic system, it does not require oxygen to create energy. It can also create energy relatively quickly (within ten seconds of starting exercise) and can operate fully for up to three to five minutes of high intensity exercise.

Unlike the aerobic system, the anaerobic energy system creates two waste products known as lactate and hydrogen ions (commonly called acid). These start to accumulate within the muscle cells and the blood stream after a few minutes. The build-up of lactate and hydrogen ions eventually creates fatigue which overwhelms the runner and causes them to slow down and stop.

The anaerobic system can be developed by a range of training methods. These include intervals sessions, fartleks and blocks of continuous running at lactate threshold.

ATP (Adenosine Triphosphate, Creatine Phosphate or ATP-CP)

The ATP system is utilised mostly for sprint events of 100–200m so has the least relevance to 5k to half marathon. But it should not be neglected entirely as it may power your sprint finish in longer events.

The ATP energy system uses adenosine triphosphate and creatine phosphate stored in the muscles to fuel short bursts of very high intensity exercise. It is an immediate energy source but the supply of ATP is also exhausted very quickly. The ATP system can usually only provide energy for two to ten seconds. After this period of time the production of energy predominantly shifts to the anaerobic system.

ATP is replenished within the muscles over time. This takes a minimum of two to three minutes and happens most quickly during periods of rest.

The ATP system is developed by short high intensity bursts of exercise with significant periods of rest to allow full recovery. This may be short sprints between two to eight seconds duration or maximal strength or power efforts in the gym.

General Components of Endurance

Rather than target training broadly at energy systems we tend to build fitness by focusing on some more specific points where we know training benefits are greater. We can call these the general components of endurance:

- Aerobic endurance
- Threshold
- VO_2 max
- Race pace

Comparison of the General Components of Endurance Running

Description	Easy	Steady	Threshold	VO_2 max	Max velocity
RPE	3/10 Easy effort. Feels comfortable and able to sustain for extended duration	3–4/10 Feels comfortable but requires some low-level conscious effort. Able to sustain for an extended duration	6/10 Conscious effort. Comfortably uncomfortable. Can sustain for 20–50 mins approx., subject to fitness	8/10 Hard effort. Working hard to sustain pace. Can sustain for up to 8–9 mins	10/10 Very hard effort. Only able to sustain for 5–10 secs
Talk test	Able to hold full conversation	Able to hold conversation	Able to say short sentence (usually 4–8 words)	Able to say 2–4 words.	Unable to speak
Percentage max HR	Less than 80%	Less than 85%	Approx. 88–92%	Approx. 95–100%	100% or above
Blood lactate	Less than 2mmol/l	Usually around 2mmol/l	Usually between 2–4mmol/l	Above 4mmol/l	Not measurable
Race pace	None applicable	Possibly up to half marathon, subject to fitness	5–10k race distance or between 10k and half marathon, subject to fitness	3k or shorter	100m sprint or less

- Anaerobic speed reserve and maximum velocity
- Strength and strength endurance

Some components are more specific to certain race distances than others. For example, VO_2 max is more closely related to 5k, threshold to 10k and aerobic endurance to half marathon. But to perform at your best across any distance, your training needs to target all of these components, albeit to differing degrees. Hence they are called the general components of endurance.

Aerobic Endurance

Aerobic endurance is the most fundamental component of endurance and underpins all others. Aerobic endurance is the ability to run at a low intensity for an extended period of time predominantly using the aerobic energy system. So it's not surprising that easy runs form the foundation of endurance training.

To maximise development of aerobic endurance it is important that easy runs are not too hard. You should be able to maintain the same easy effort for the whole duration of the run without the need to slow down or work harder.

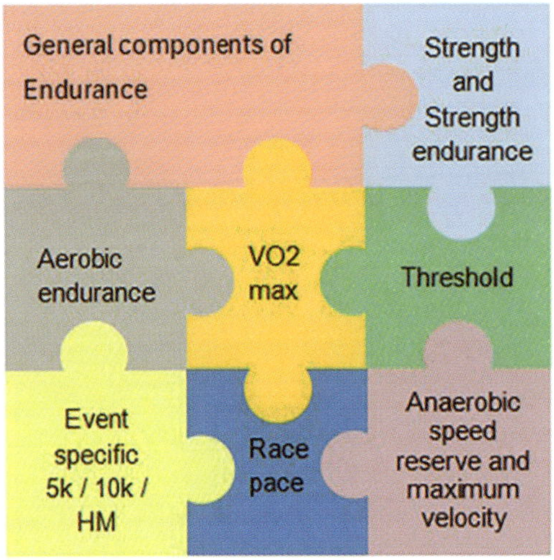

Several components of fitness are required for endurance running.

In practice this means easy runs should always be significantly slower than your 5k, 10k and half marathon pace. Although breathing rate is increased, you should be able to comfortably hold a conversation. Heart rate should be stable and usually between 60 and 85 per cent maximum heart rate.

Long runs are extended easy runs and help to improve running economy as well as endurance. Running economy is the amount of energy it takes to run at any set pace over any set period. The better your running economy the less oxygen you use for the same effort. Running economy is improved through these physical adaptations:

- Strengthening the heart to increase the volume of blood pumped in each beat, which increases oxygen transported to muscles
- Increasing the number of capillaries within the muscles, which increases blood volume and oxygen absorption in the muscles (known as capillarisation)
- Increasing the number and function of mitochondria in muscles that convert oxygen into energy

Threshold

Lactate threshold is also known as anaerobic threshold or lactate turning point 2. It is the physiological point where you start to move from predominantly using the aerobic energy system towards a greater proportion of energy being created through the anaerobic energy system.

As we discussed earlier in this chapter, lactate is one of the waste products created by the anaerobic energy system. Contrary to popular belief, lactate is important as it is both a waste product and a source of energy in its own right. Threshold is the maximum intensity at which you can maintain relatively stable levels of blood lactate by converting lactate back into energy.

Above this level lactate then starts to accumulate exponentially in the muscles and blood. Some physiologists and coaches prefer the term 'maximum metabolic steady state' to lactate threshold as it is a more accurate description of the wider range of significant metabolic markers involved. However, lactate is the most well known of the metabolic markers and the commonly used measure.

The pace you can run at threshold and how long you can run at that pace before you need to slow down (your capacity to sustain threshold pace) are key components of endurance. More importantly, they are very strongly correlated with potential performance in 5k to half marathon.

The more you train around threshold, the more efficient you become at re-utilising lactate back into energy and the longer you can hold this pace. Newer runners may only be able to maintain their threshold pace for ten to fifteen minutes. Well-trained and elite runners can maintain their threshold pace for 40 to 60 minutes. The good news for Masters runners is that threshold training remains highly effective for older runners (unlike VO_2 max scores, which decline significantly with age as we will discuss next).

As we touched on earlier in Chapter 1, the most accurate way to measure threshold is using lactate blood monitors. However, for most of us this is invasive and impractical for day-to-day training. As an easier alternative, threshold pace tends to be between your 5k and half marathon pace, subject to fitness. For less well-trained or slower runners this may be closer to 5k to 10k pace (30–35min or slower for 5k). For more well-trained or faster runners it will be closer to 10k to half marathon pace.

Threshold effort is commonly described as being 'comfortably uncomfortable' (RPE 6). Your breathing should be relatively elevated but not gasping and you should be able to say five or six words. Heart rate should be able to remain stable at approx. 88–92 per cent max HR.

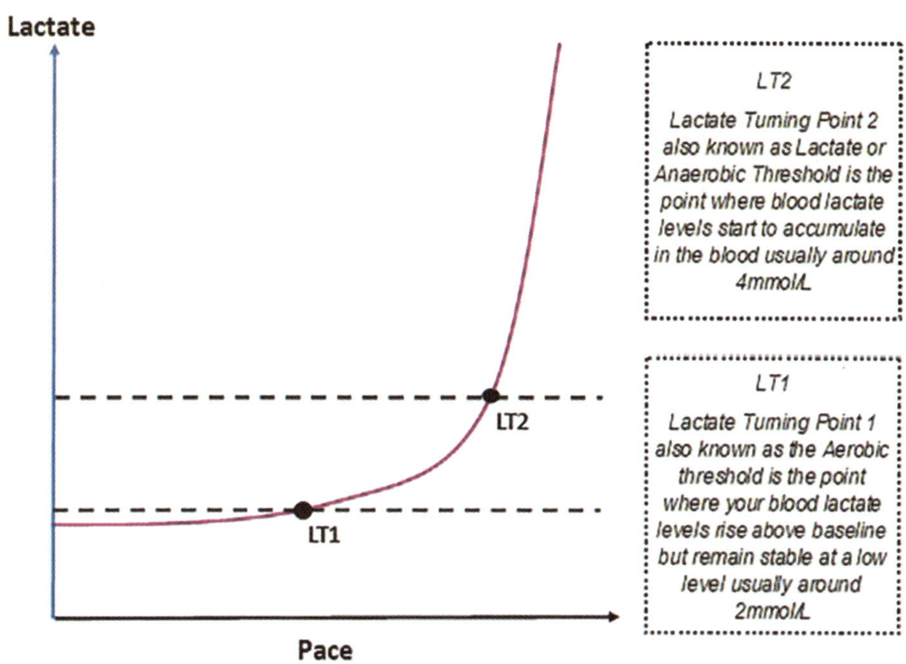

The lactate curve shows the increase in blood lactate levels associated with increase in pace and intensity of effort.

Threshold training usually comprises longer continuous blocks of running at threshold, long or short threshold intervals or threshold fartleks (where you aim to run alternatively just under and just over threshold).

VO_2 max

VO_2 max is the maximum quantity of oxygen (in millilitres) per minute per kilogram of bodyweight that you can breathe in and process into energy. As you run faster your energy demand increases and your breathing rate goes up to enable you to breathe as much oxygen as possible. However, you reach a point (VO_2 max) where you cannot process any more oxygen even if you run faster.

VO_2 max scores can be predicted by a range of formulas and fitness devices. However, VO_2 max can only be measured accurately by specialist equipment in a sports science laboratory that measures the volume of oxygen inhaled against the volume of oxygen exhaled.

It is commonly accepted that VO_2 max score is a very good predictor of sports performance and elite athletes or faster runners usually have high VO_2 max scores. Males usually have a higher score than females due to differences in body composition including bigger heart and lung capacity.

Unfortunately for Masters runners, VO_2 max is known to decline significantly with age. This is due to a number of age-related factors including decline in muscular strength of the heart and lungs, lower density of capillaries and loss of efficiency in mitochondria.

Newer runners can achieve significant increases in VO_2 max, but for most Masters runners it is not worth seeking to arbitrarily increase your VO_2 max score as an outcome in its own right. That said, you should not neglect training at VO_2 max pace and intensity as it remains an important component of endurance for Masters runners.

Most runners can only sustain VO_2 max pace for up to eight or nine minutes, which makes it significantly faster than 5k pace. VO_2 max requires serious effort (usually 8–9 RPE). Your breathing should be significantly increased and you can usually only say three or four words at most. Your heart rate should be around 95 to 98 per cent maximum heart rate.

VO_2 max is developed by running fast intervals and good quality strength work including, more specifically, plyometrics. At the other end of the scale VO_2 max is also improved by improvements in running economy from long runs.

Anaerobic Speed Reserve and Maximum Velocity

Anaerobic speed reserve is the gap between the pace at VO_2 max and the fastest pace you can run, known as your maximum velocity. It's fair to say that anaerobic speed reserve and maximum velocity are not strictly components of endurance and they are not particularly relevant to 5k, 10k or half marathon.

For Masters runners there is more benefit in training to minimise general age-related declines in strength and power (discussed in greater detail in Chapter 3) more than specifically focusing on max velocity speed. However, more competitive runners may wish to do some work to develop these speed components to develop their sprint finish, power and general running technique.

Anaerobic speed reserve and maximum velocity predominantly rely on the ATP and anaerobic energy systems. They are developed by speedwork and sprint training. Speedwork is used in its purest form here to refer to short, very fast intervals usually over 30–200 metres with very long recovery. Weights, strength work, power exercises, plyometrics and jumps are all equally important methods.

Strength and Strength Endurance

Strength is more commonly associated with speed and power events such as sprints and throws. However, increased strength means you generate more force with each step.

Strength training enables you to recruit more muscle fibres and strength endurance trains those muscle fibres to work for longer before they become fatigued. Plyometric exercises help you to maintain the elastic properties of the tendons. All of these components reduce the energy cost of running and help you to run faster for longer.

As we have discussed, strength training is important for Masters runners, especially for female runners. Greater strength minimises age-related loss of muscular strength, improves robustness and potentially enables you to increase your total running volume, which will significantly improve performance.

Strength and strength endurance are developed through strength workouts, which include bodyweight exercises, heavy weights, resistance bands, jumps and plyometric exercises.

How Training Works and the Key Principles of Training

Now you are familiar with the key components of endurance it's helpful to understand how training works. Over many years as an athlete, I built an implicit understanding of training principles. You do some training. Then about four to eight weeks later you get much fitter. Unbeknown to me, this was the key principle of adaptation, which is important because fundamentally it governs how training works from what you do to when you do it.

The Principle of Adaptation

The principle of adaptation describes the process by which the body makes physiological adaptations in response to a training stimulus and explains how training makes you fitter.

Training stimulus is running or strength work or another form of activity (muscular, neurological or metabolic) that puts the body under stress. This stress must challenge the body enough to create some fatigue. In response, the body makes physiological adaptations that enable it to cope better with future similar activity or training load. In simple terms, you get faster, stronger or can run for longer.

However, it's important to understand that adaptation relies on recovery as much as training. Which leads us on to the second key principle.

Recovery

Contrary to common misperception, adaptation happens in the period of recovery *after* and not during training. Without sufficient recovery there is only limited or no adaptation. That means you do not fully benefit from the running or training that you have done and just accumulate fatigue instead. Recovery is fundamentally important for Masters runners.

As we age, muscle repair and regeneration is less efficient and the body takes longer to recover. This is the main reason why most Masters runners should not put hard training sessions back to back. It also limits how many hard workouts Masters runners can realistically complete per week.

But recovery is not just about rest from training. It's important not to overlook the practical impact of lifestyle factors on recovery. Those in their forties and fifties are more likely to have a greater range of demands on their time, energy and emotional reserves. These might include everything that comes with work and professional commitments, alongside significant family commitments such as caring for young children and older parents. This is also the age when sleep may start to be more interrupted or limited, especially for women during the menopause.

Progressive Overload

Progressive overload explains why training must be regular and repeated to create significant and lasting adaptations. The number of training stimuli per week and the number of weeks required varies subject to the nature of the adaptation you want.

In practice, this usually means three to four runs or running sessions per week or more, which is why this book (and most training plans) include this number of runs as a minimum. Note that you can still get fit on less than three runs per week, but the process of adaptation takes longer as the stimulus is less frequent.

The principle of progressive overload also governs why training should be gradually increased in duration, volume, intensity or frequency as the body gets used to each training load. This implies that in theory you should continually make training harder, faster or longer to continue to improve. But we also know that Masters runners need more recovery and must balance training against age-related physical decline, which means it's often not possible to do more training. So how do Masters runners continue to improve as they get older? This is the concept of Training Age and it's great news for many Masters runners.

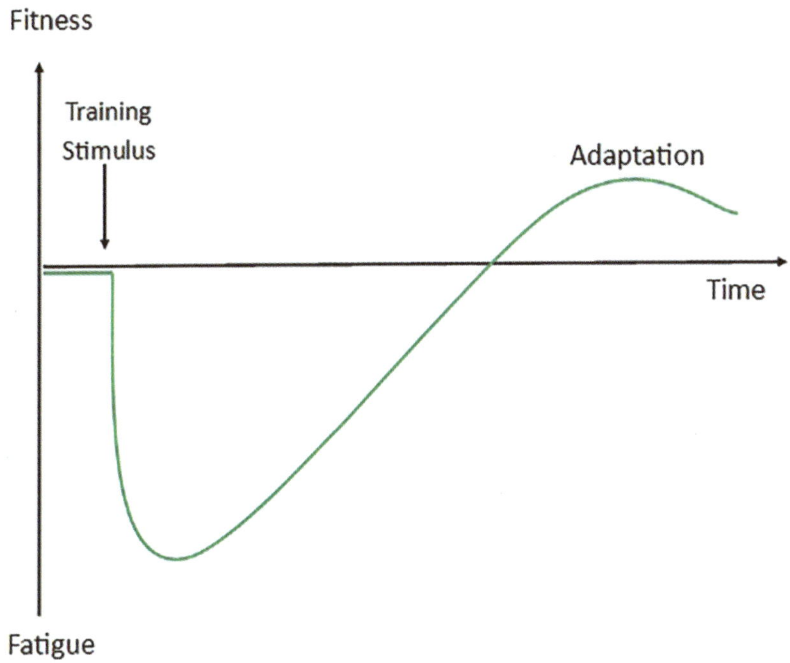

The principle of adaptation describes how the body makes physiological adaptations in response to training stimulus to improve fitness.

Training Age

Chronological age is literally how old you are, whereas training age refers to the number of years you have been training. If you have only been training for a short period of time, for example less than two years, then your training age is low.

The basic principle of progressive overload determines that as we stack one training cycle on top of another, we improve fitness. For Masters runners this means if their training age is low then their capacity to make adaptations and improve significantly outweighs the negative impact of age-related decline through chronological age. This is particularly the case if they are starting from a low base of fitness.

Even if Masters runners have been training for many years, adding a new stimulus to their training may still enable further improvements in performance. This could be intervals sessions, strength work or more volume. They could also change

There is this new guy in my club who had never run in his life before. He's only been running two or three years now. He's getting faster and faster. I said to him last week, 'Blooming heck, Colin, you did really well'. He's only a year younger than me at 67 but I suspect he's going to be beating me soon.

John

Adaptation only happens during the period of recovery.

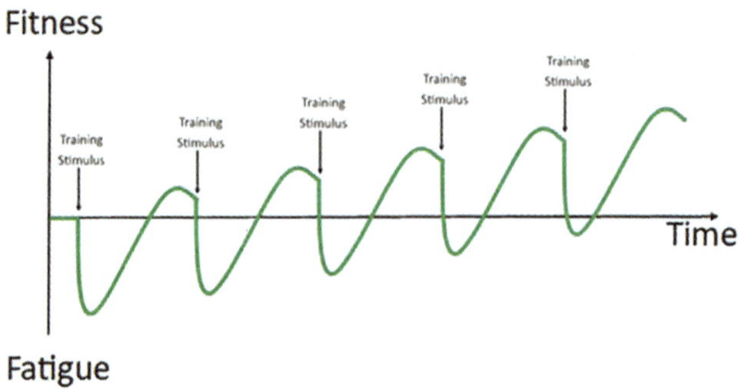

Progressive overload occurs when one training cycle follows another to build fitness incrementally.

focus, for example by switching from shorter to longer events or vice versa. This explains why many older, more experienced runners decide to tackle new distances often with great success.

Overtraining

However, regardless of training age, progressive overload must still always be balanced with appropriate recovery. Otherwise, this leads to overtraining.

Overtraining is when you overload the body so that it cannot make the adaptations you hope. This might be because the training load is too high (too much or too soon), you have insufficient recovery, or cumulative fatigue becomes too great.

In practical terms the result of overtraining is that you fail to improve, potentially start running more slowly (supposedly for 'no apparent reason') or, worst of all, become injured or ill.

The only effective way to manage overtraining is to step back and allow more time for rest and recovery. However, no runner likes enforced rest as we all start to fear that we will get unfit. That leads nicely to the principle of detraining and more pertinently to dispelling another myth.

Detraining

Detraining is the opposite process to adaptation. If the training load decreases or stops then the body gradually returns to its untrained state. This is often described as 'use it or lose it'. But this must be balanced against the fundamental importance of recovery, as we have already discussed, especially if this fear of detraining leads to reluctance to take much needed rest and recovery breaks.

It is worth reminding yourself that detraining happens at a much slower rate than we think. So whilst extended breaks or repeated neglect of specific aspects of fitness will eventually lead to some detraining, if you need to rest to manage illness, injury or general fatigue, then you are not going to lose significant fitness.

Timescales for Adaptation

Just as we don't lose fitness overnight, we cannot build fitness overnight either. Each type of adaptation has a slightly different timescale. These help you plan when and where to put each training session into your plan.

What Helps Adaptation?

There is a whole industry that has grown up around things that promise to help you to get fitter quicker or recover faster. But do they work?

The two factors that have the biggest positive impact on adaptation are also the simplest: sleep and good nutrition. Our body undertakes most of the process of repair and regeneration during sleep. The bad news is that quality of sleep often deteriorates with age. The impact of hormones during the menopause and underlying health conditions increase rates of insomnia and sleeplessness amongst older athletes. So as a Masters runner, prioritising sufficient time to sleep is important to get the most from your training.

As I've got older I really struggle with insomnia and I lie awake all night. I've learnt that I need to be honest when I've not slept. I still have to go to work but I have to cut back running as otherwise that is when I end up injured.

Sam

Nutrition is very important in terms of both what and when you eat. You should aim to eat as soon as possible after training. Protein is essential to promote tissue repair and carbohydrate starts the process of replenishing energy stores. One of the most simple and effective ways to refuel after training is to drink a pint of cow's milk. For non-dairy diets you will need to be aware that alternative milk drinks have very different quantities of protein and carbohydrate, so you will need to check the label. (For more information *see* Chapter 5.)

What Hinders Adaptation?

Conversely lack of sleep, poor nutrition and lack of refuelling significantly limits adaptation. Alcohol consumption has a particularly negative effect.

Ice baths are growing in popularity as cold water works to ease sore muscles by dampening inflammation. However, it is also argued that the inflammatory response to exercise is important to trigger the body to make adaptations. The general consensus is that whilst ice baths make you feel

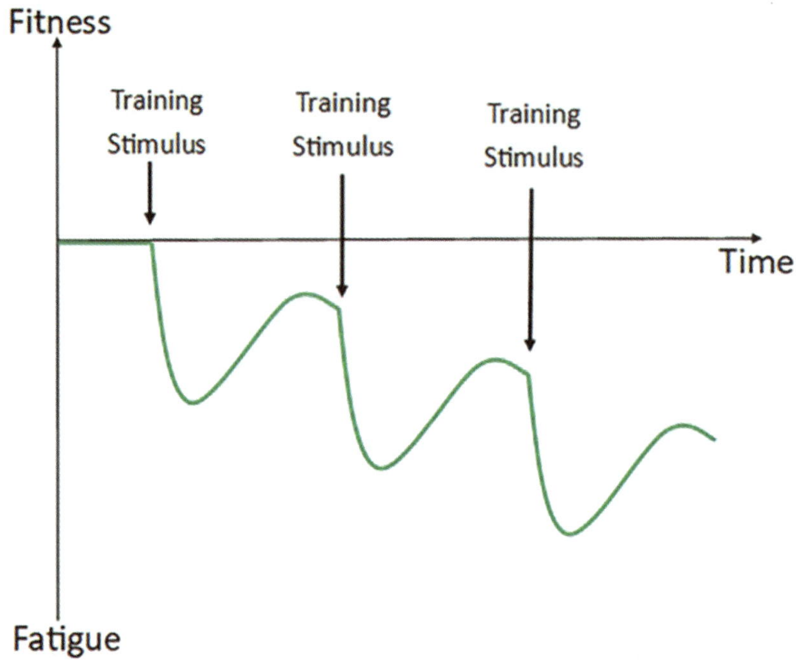

Overtraining happens when training is too hard or there is insufficient recovery.

Key Timescales for Adaptation

Adaptation	Description	Frequency of training load	Timescale for initial adaptation
Aerobic energy system	Increases in volume of blood pumped per beat and oxygen concentration in blood. Lower resting heart rate and more efficient heart function	3–6 × per week	6–8 weeks
	Increase in number of capillaries, number and function of mitochondria in muscles	3–6 × per week	Up to 1 year
Anaerobic energy system	Greater stores of glycogen and improved function of mitochondria. Improved lactate buffering capacity within the muscle	1 × week	6–8 weeks
ATP energy system	Increased stores of ATP and creatine in muscles. Improved neuromuscular pathways	1 × week	8–12 weeks
Muscle adaptation	Change in size and volume of muscle fibres	2–3 × per week	3–4 weeks
Tendons	Improvement in strength of tendons and elasticity	2–3 × per week	8–12 weeks
Bone	Improved bone health and increased bone density	2–3 × per week	8–12 weeks

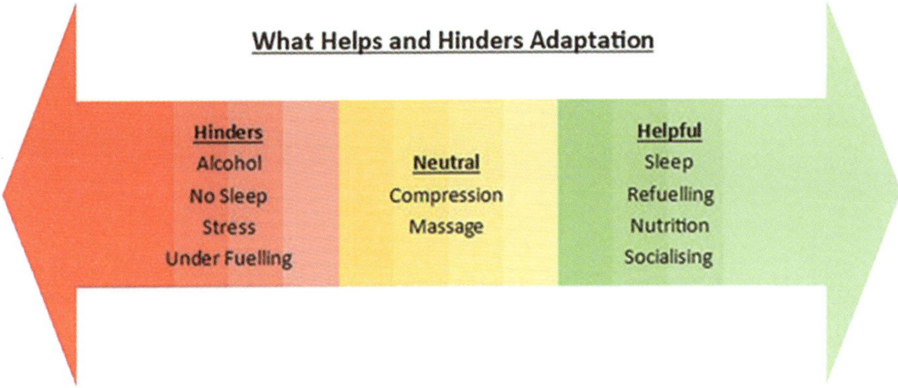

Several key factors help or hinder the process of adaptation.

refreshed and less sore within your general day-to-day training, they should be used sparingly.

Other common practices have a more neutral effect on adaptation. Massage is claimed to help improve blood flow to the muscles and potentially clear waste products. There is no absolutely definitive evidence of the effectiveness of massage on adaptation, but as massage tends to create calm and relaxation it may be positive in other ways. Similarly, it's claimed that compression helps blood flow to the limbs, but there is no definitive evidence that it encourages adaptation. Both massage and compression may just provide a placebo effect. But if they make you feel stronger, fitter and faster, or just feel good, then go ahead.

7 Training Runs and Training Sessions

Now we have considered the key concepts and principles it is time to consider what they look like in practice. Each training plan is like a jigsaw puzzle made up of these different types of runs and workouts which, when they are all put together, build the bigger picture.

This chapter considers all of the key runs and training sessions for 5k, 10k and half marathon as well as exploring what the key points are for each one.

Easy Run

Easy runs are the foundation of most training plans and (subject to your current training block) should make up between 60 and 100 per cent of your total weekly running volume.

Long Run

To state the obvious, your long run should be the longest run you do each week. Long runs are extended easy runs that improve your endurance by increasing the period of time that you can sustain this relaxed aerobic effort.

How Long Is Long?

It's important to remember that long runs should only be as long as the duration for which you can maintain the required effort. If you need to slow down dramatically or take significant walk breaks, or if your heart rate starts to drift upwards towards the end of your long runs, these may be signs that your long run is too long right now.

I love the variety of training and running over the weeks, months and years. Easy runs, mixed pace runs, different types of fartleks and intervals sessions and for me especially the one I look forward to most is my long run.

Hervé

Endurance is built most effectively when the long run is supported by a medium length run rather than being disproportionately long in comparison to your other runs. In practice your long run should be no more than 30 per cent longer than your next longest run.

If you are training for 5k or 10k then ideally your long run should be longer than your target race. If you are training for half marathon then ideally you should aim to build your long run up to 20km or above over time. More guidance on how to increase your long runs is included in Chapter 10.

What Pace is My Long Run?

Aerobic endurance comes mostly from the duration rather than the pace of your long run. This makes long runs an excellent way to practise pace judgement and discipline. If you need to slow down in the latter stages or the perceived level of effort to maintain the same pace starts to increase, or your heart rate drifts upwards, then you need to start more slowly next time.

Running too fast or too hard on the long run not only decreases the desired training benefits and adaptations but also increases your risk of injury. It should take you no more than one or two days at most to recover from your long run, otherwise you start to jeopardise your upcoming runs if you are too tired to run them properly.

Mental Training Benefits of Long Runs

Long runs also help you to develop concentration and focus over an extended period alongside resilience and determination. Unlike shorter runs, you are more likely to find that you go through both good and bad patches during your long run. These are useful training opportunities to practise positive self-talk and other techniques for determination (*see* Chapter 1).

Are You a 'Watch Stopper'?

It's helpful to take note how many times you stop your watch on your long run. Some runners like to stop their watch for pragmatic reasons such as to cross roads, tie shoelaces or go to the toilet.

As you build fitness and increase the distance of your long run, you may feel you need to stop your watch more frequently to take a break. A few brief stops should not overly affect the training benefit from your run but you should keep an eye on your overall elapsed time.

If the total time on rest breaks starts to creep up above a few minutes then you should consider if you need to build up your fitness before you add further distance to your long run.

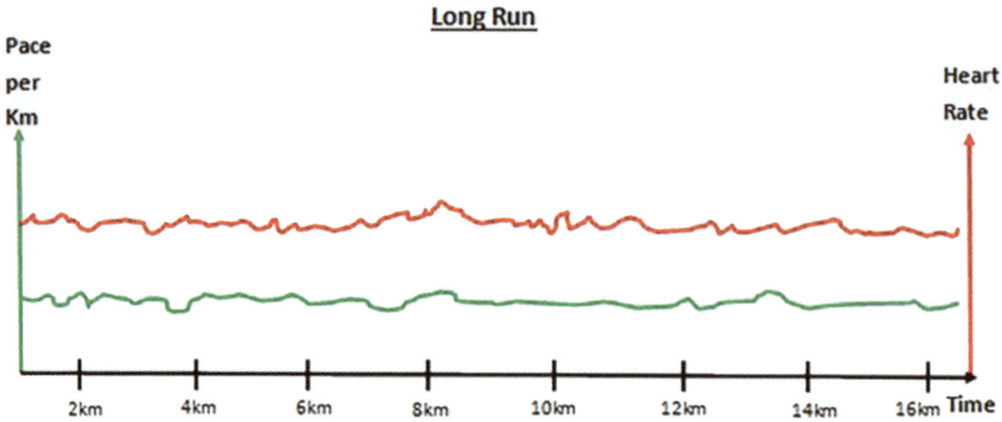

Long runs should be evenly paced with no increase in effort or heart rate.

Some runners like to listen to music whilst others prefer not. This is very much a personal choice, but you should note that some races do not permit headphones, so if possible you should ensure you do some runs without music to prepare.

Mixed Pace Long Runs

Mixed pace long runs combine long runs with blocks of faster running similar to an extended intervals session. They are a very good way to build specific fitness for half marathons. They are more challenging than easy pace long runs and require a better base of fitness. Before you tackle a mixed pace long run you should always first ensure you can comfortably run the total distance at an easy pace.

> **Example 18km mixed pace long run**
> - 1km easy jog warm up
> - 4 × (3km easy pace, 1km half marathon pace)
> - 1km easy jog cool-down

Mixed pace long runs also challenge you to be disciplined and pace yourself well from the start. If the easy sections are too fast you will struggle to lift the pace as required in the faster sections or struggle to complete the whole run.

Strides

Strides are short bursts of faster but comfortable, controlled running where the aim is to focus on form not pace. They should be run on feel rather than set pace, although in practice they are likely to be around 5k to 10k pace or faster.

Strides have traditionally been part of the warm-up. However, they can also be very effective to add to the end of an easy run. This helps you with some additional focus on form and how you run. It also helps

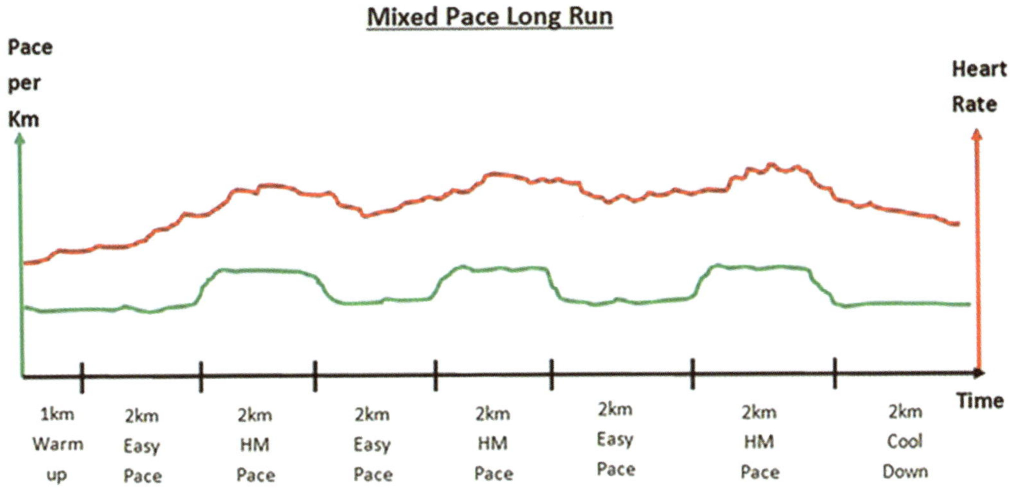

Mixed pace long runs, such as this example covering 15km, have blocks of half marathon pace within them and are specific training for half marathons.

inject some pace and improve leg turnover without adding too much fatigue.

Strides should focus on these key points:

- Good posture (stand up 'tall', lift through hips and tuck in core)
- Relaxed shoulders
- Strong backwards arm drive
- Relaxed hands
- Conscious but natural knee lift
- Short ground contact

Strides should usually be 100 to 200 metres or approximately 15 to 20 seconds. Accelerate gradually, hold this pace over the distance required and then gently decelerate before you stop. Walk or jog back or take 30–90 seconds recovery.

Surges

Surges are essentially extended strides usually lasting between 30 and 60 seconds. As with strides, their purpose is to focus on form not fitness. Surges are useful to bridge the gap between easy runs and faster sessions if you are relatively new to running, have limited experience of running intervals sessions, or after significant periods of injury.

Surges also work well inserted into one or two easy runs each week as a regular part of training. They can help you to feel 'sharp' and break up the slow and sluggish feeling that can sometimes arise from just doing easy runs. They also allow you to put additional focus onto how you run.

Easy Run with Surges

These are repeated short blocks of easy running (usually 10 minutes) followed by 2 × 60 seconds surges, with 60 seconds gentle jog or walk recovery. This is repeated for the set number of times. Ideally the whole run should flow continuously with no additional recovery. If you feel that you need more recovery then slow down on either the surges or on the easy run pace.

Easy Run with Block of Surges

These are usually two longer blocks of easy running (between 10 and 25 minutes) with one block of 5 × 60 seconds surges, with 60 seconds recovery in the middle. As above, you should be able to maintain a continuous flow without the need for any additional recovery.

Progression Runs

Progression runs are runs that start easy and gradually get faster. They may be structured or unstructured. Structured runs might include blocks of time or distance, such as a 3 × 15 minutes progression run where each block of 15 minutes is run at a set pace faster than the previous block, or a 5k progression run where each kilometre is run faster than the previous kilometre. Unstructured progression runs are where you start easy and naturally allow yourself to run faster as you go along.

Progression runs can be excellent ways to practise pace judgement and discipline and enable you to hit a range of training paces and intensities in one session. You very quickly learn that if you start too fast you will not reach the desired pace at the end of the run. Progression runs are also a highly effective way of managing overall training load because most of the run is easy to medium effort until the final stages of the run.

Intervals Sessions

If easy runs are the foundations, then intervals sessions are the bricks and mortar. Intervals sessions are blocks of faster

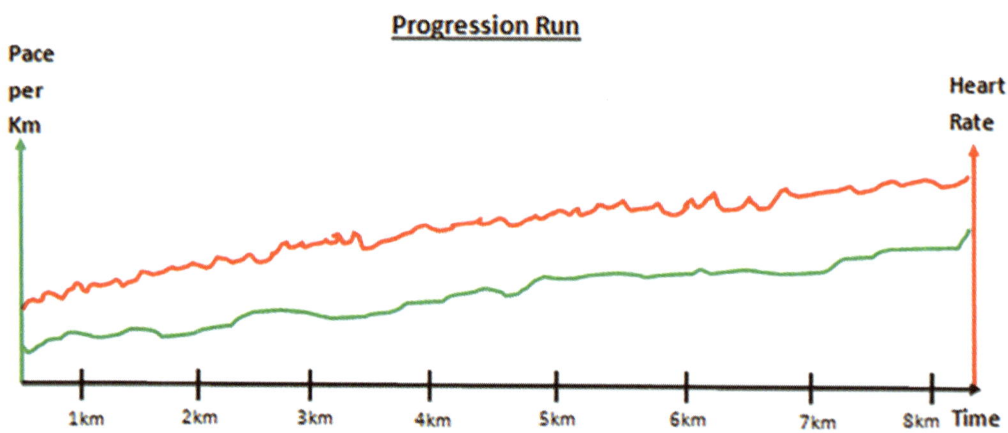

During progression runs the pace should gradually increase from easy to medium to hard effort.

> *I love intervals sessions. I see them as a game. Can I push myself hard enough that I am tired at the end but not too much that I have to slow down in the last few.*
>
> Hervé

running broken up with periods of rest or recovery. They are usually described in terms of reps and possibly sets and may be measured in time or distance.

The beauty of interval sessions is that you can change the training focus, load and desired adaptations of each session just by changing one or more of the key variables. In this way intervals sessions allow you to develop the different components of endurance in a multitude of different ways.

- Volume is the total amount of running in the session when you add together all the intervals.
- Duration is the length of each rep or interval. These may be standard across the whole session or vary.
- Pace or intensity is how fast to run.
- Recovery is the rest period between each interval described in terms of duration, distance and nature.

Volume

Changing the overall volume is the most obvious adjustment to any training session: 12 × 2 minutes reps (24 minutes) increases training load from 9 × 2 minutes reps (18 minutes).

Adding volume is the simplest way to add progression to your session. But there are more subtle and effective ways to manipulate the key components to change your training load.

Duration

Altering the duration of reps changes the training focus to make it more or less physically and mentally challenging: 9 × 2 minutes and 6 × 3 minutes are both 18 minutes of volume, but 3 minutes reps are potentially physically harder because you must hold the same effort per rep for 50 per cent longer.

Longer reps can also be more mentally challenging than short reps as they demand more focus and longer concentration. For example, many runners would find 2 × 9 minutes psychologically much harder than 9 × 2 minutes, even if they were run at the same or slower pace.

Pace

Out of all the variables, pace is the key component that determines the training focus of each interval session. If we consider 9 × 2 minutes again, there is a significant difference in training load and difficulty between 5k pace reps and half marathon pace reps.

Running intervals sessions at the right pace is important not only to maximise training benefits but also to develop important skills in discipline and pace judgement.

Recovery

Recovery is the final key component that determines the intended training benefits from any intervals session. Often it is what determines the toughness of the session. Recovery can be passive rest, easy walk, jog or faster pace running (often described as a float). The role of the recovery is to maintain or improve the quality of the effort and extend the overall time you can spend working at the required intensity.

For example, you may only be able to hold your VO_2 max capacity for four or five minutes in one continuous run. Breaking the overall effort into intervals with recovery may allow you to accumulate 15–20 minutes at the required capacity, multiplying the training stimulus.

However, be warned it also works the other way. The greater the recovery between the intervals, the easier the session becomes, which risks diluting the training stimulus instead.

Start from Where You are Now

One of the most common mistakes in intervals sessions is to do too much too soon. It's great to 'train like an elite' and try some big sessions every now and then. But it's also important to be realistic.

If the session is too long, too fast or has insufficient recovery, you will not be able to complete the whole session as intended. Potentially, you won't get the desired adaptions or, worse, you will become demoralised or overtrain.

The key question is 'Can you run the whole session at the pace and effort level required with the set recovery?' If the answer is 'no', then you need to build up progressively in terms of volume, duration of reps, pace or recovery until you can.

Don't Rush Progression

The second most common mistake in intervals sessions is to add progression too quickly. The timescale for aerobic and anaerobic adaptation is six to eight weeks. The timescales for improvements in strength in muscles, tendons and ligaments are two to three months and up to a year to develop changes in density of capillaries and mitochondria in muscles.

Progression in sessions should match these timescales and ideally you should not progress a session until you can achieve the intended targets or training outcomes. In any case, session progress should rarely occur any more frequently than every four to six weeks.

Only change one element of the session each time: either recovery, pace or number of reps. This will help you build fitness more effectively within your programme. It also helps you identify what works most effectively for you, so that you can develop further.

But Don't Forget to Add More

This is the opposite problem to adding too much too soon. It can be tempting to sit in your comfort zone and not challenge yourself. Intervals are by their very nature harder than easy runs. They take mental focus and determination to push yourself at

Guide to Key Variables in Intervals Sessions

Total volume	Pace or intensity	Duration of reps	Recovery required	Possible progressions	Energy system
15–60min	Threshold or below	1–20min	Usually short recovery. May be active recovery from easy jog to medium pace jog/run 30sec to 5min, subject to length of reps	Increase volume Increase duration of reps Decrease recovery Increase intensity of recovery from easy jog to float or medium effort run	Mostly aerobic
15–40min	5k–10k pace	1–10min for 10k pace 1–6min for 5k pace	Requires greater recovery, especially 5k pace. 30sec to 5min, subject to length of reps. May be broken into sets to maintain quality of pace	Increase overall volume Increase duration of reps Decrease recovery	Aerobic and anaerobic
10–20min	VO_2 max	30sec to 5min	Recovery usually 1:1 ratio with duration of reps to allow sufficient recovery	Increase duration of reps Decrease recovery Increase pace	Anaerobic with some aerobic stimulus
2–10min maximum	Max velocity	10–60sec maximum	Significant recovery required. Usually 1:4 ratio length of rep to recovery or 2–3min minimum up to 10min	Increase pace	ATP and Anaerobic

the required intensity. If your sessions are too easy, they will not provide sufficient training stimulus to improve fitness. A session may be too easy because it lacks sufficient pace, volume or has too much recovery.

However, sometimes you may think the session is too easy when it is actually spot on. Threshold sessions come to mind here. Threshold is a disciplined and controlled effort, but the training benefit of the session is diluted if you run too much harder. So make sure you understand the intended training benefits of each session.

Fartlek

Fartlek is a Swedish word which means 'speed play'. Fartlek sessions are blocks of continuous mixed pace running. They may be structured or unstructured. They differ slightly from intervals in that they are always continuous, whereas intervals may have passive rest or recovery. Fartleks have a range of training purposes and for this book they are divided into easy fartleks and threshold fartleks.

Easy Fartleks

Easy fartleks build general fitness with less mental or physical pressure as there is no set pace or distance. They can be an excellent way to rebuild fitness after interruptions for illness or injury. They are also very good as a bridge into sessions if you have limited experience of intervals sessions, as long as you do not run them too hard.

Ideally in easy fartleks you decide how fast to run each effort and each recovery based on how you feel on the day and your current level of fitness. Each effort may vary in length and intensity throughout. You can run easy fartleks off road on varied terrain, trail or parkland. This enables you to use the terrain to guide your effort more appropriately. For example you might put more effort in uphill or take your recovery by running downhill.

Example Easy Fartlek

- 2–3 × 10min easy fartlek (either your choice or 1 min medium to good effort, 90sec easy effort)
- 2min recovery between blocks

Threshold Fartleks

In contrast to easy fartleks, threshold fartleks are very specific sessions to improve pace at lactate threshold and lactate tolerance as well as extend your capacity to run at threshold for longer. The pace is a mix of good efforts that are just above threshold pace and steady 'recovery' efforts, which should be just below threshold.

In these sessions, the desired training benefit arises from the steady sections more than the faster sections and it is important that these do not slow down too much. This challenges you to process lactate back into

Example Threshold Fartlek

- Continuous 4–6 ×
- 2min 30sec (10k pace)
- 2min 30sec (medium effort)

energy whilst still working at a relatively high intensity.

For more competitive runners, threshold fartleks are also highly effective specific training sessions to mimic mid-race surges (and the consequent sudden increase in lactate levels) common in highly competitive 5k to 10k races.

Threshold Training Sessions

Threshold training sessions are designed to improve your capacity to run at threshold. This means your pace at threshold and the duration for which you can hold this pace. Threshold sessions include short, mid-length and long intervals, blocks of threshold running or continuous threshold runs.

Short Threshold Reps

Short threshold reps are very short intervals with very short recovery. They are usually run slightly faster than threshold pace. The short duration allows you to run faster whilst not building up significant lactate levels. The short recovery means that in practice your heart rate remains relatively stable around threshold. Mentally they can feel easier than longer threshold reps or continuous threshold runs. They are also helpful if your capacity to hold your threshold effort is not well developed.

Mid-Length Threshold Reps

Mid-length threshold reps are usually between three and six minutes. They have a short recovery, which requires you to be disciplined in your pace judgement to ensure that it is sustained. They are very effective to help you to accumulate more time at threshold than might be possible if you were running a continuous threshold run. This is especially the case if your capacity to sustain your threshold is not well developed.

Example Mid-Length Threshold Reps

- 5–8 × 3min 30sec threshold reps (10k to half marathon pace)
- 1 min recovery

Long Threshold Blocks

Long threshold blocks are the stepping stone between threshold reps and continuous threshold runs. They help develop focus and capacity to maintain this effort for longer. As they are longer, the pace should be very disciplined and for most runners this should ideally be between your 10k and half marathon pace.

Example Long Threshold Blocks

- 2–3 × 10min threshold blocks (half marathon pace)
- 2min recovery

Continuous Threshold Runs

Continuous threshold runs are exactly what they say: sustained and continuous blocks of threshold pace running. They can be mentally quite challenging and require a good base of fitness and capacity to run at threshold before you can run them

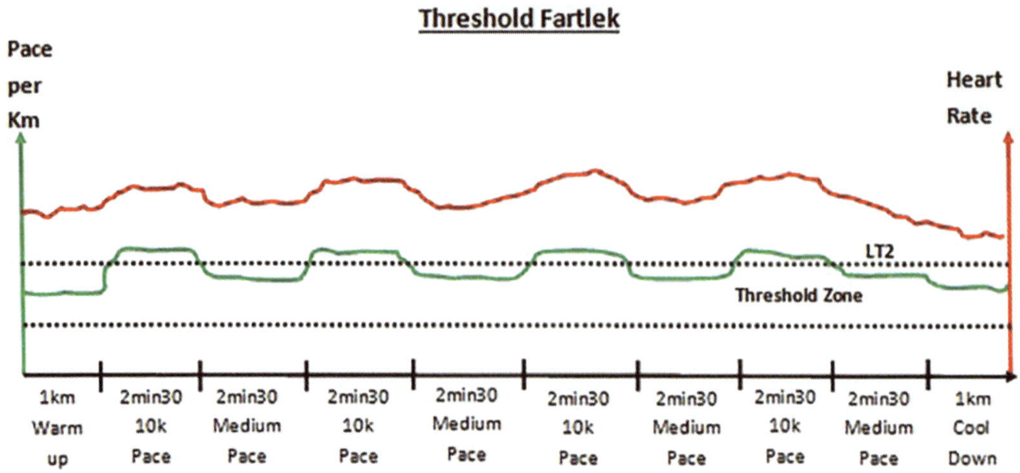

Threshold fartleks are specific sessions to improve pace at lactate threshold. The pace should go between just above threshold pace to just below.

successfully in training. However, they are very specific to 5k to half marathon and highly effective training sessions to improve your times.

Example Continuous Threshold Run

- 15–40 mins threshold run (half marathon pace)

Blended Intervals Sessions

Blended intervals sessions are intervals sessions with more than one key focus. They usually combine two or more general components of endurance. This may be threshold and faster pace intervals, or race pace intervals that work from half marathon to 10k to 5k pace.

Example Blended Intervals Sessions

- 5–10min threshold block (half marathon pace)
- 2min recovery
- 3–6 × 2min reps (VO_2 max pace)
- 2min recovery between reps
- 3–5 × 30sec hard effort
- 1 min recovery

Pyramid Session

A pyramid session is a specific type of blended intervals session with intervals that either get longer or shorter or both. The pace should also get faster as the intervals get shorter or slower as they get longer to work through the range of training paces in one session.

Example Pyramid Session

- 1 min, 2min, 3min, 4min, 5min, 4min, 3min, 2min, 1min reps
- (VO_2 max pace to 10k to half marathon pace and back)
- 90sec recovery between reps

Track Sessions

Track sessions are essentially intervals session that are based on the track. They are measured in distance rather than time. The recovery may also be measured in distance or time.

Example Track Session

- 2–3 sets
- 1,000m (5k pace)
- 600m (VO_2 max pace)
- 400m (fast)
- 200m (fast)
- 90sec recovery between reps
- 3–4min between sets

Hills

Hill sessions are intervals sessions run up and sometimes up and down hill. Running uphill is harder than running on the flat as it requires you to work against gravity. This means hills can be good to develop both fitness and leg strength.

Hills also help to develop good running technique as they encourage improved foot placement, better hip extension and knee drive. Downhill running can work on faster leg turnover. Some caution should be adopted around faster downhill running as it places significant additional load on hips and knees.

The structure of a hills session varies greatly, subject to the aims of the session. Steep hills develop greater strength as they require more power to drive the body uphill. Short hills work on speed, whereas longer hills develop better endurance.

The downhill recovery may be walk, jog or run, subject to the training focus. An easy walk or jog recovery puts the training focus onto the uphill effort similar to traditional intervals sessions. In contrast, continuous hill sessions with fast jog or run downhill are closer to fartlek sessions with the focus on lactate recycling in the higher intensity recovery.

The key focus of all hill sessions is to maintain the same consistent effort for the duration of the hill, so they are excellent practise of pace discipline. The common mistake is to set off too hard and then struggle to maintain that same effort to the top.

Example Hills Sessions

Short and long hills

- 4–8 × 2min hills
- 3–4min easy jog down recovery
- 4–8 × 30sec hills
- 90sec to 2min easy jog down recovery

Continuous hills

- 20–30min continuous hills
- 1–2min hills (medium to good effort)
- same time run recovery downhill

8 Managing Interruptions for Injury, Illness or Other Causes

Probably time for a training update ... Current situation is there is no training. Like an addict who thinks one little hit can't hurt, I ran a few little extra miles here and there, a bit further and a bit faster, some long runs, an old favourite training session and some even longer runs. Before I know it, I'm high on adrenalin, the wind in my hair, the miles pounding out from beneath my feet and I'm really flying! Until like the addict I OD again and I'm back on rock bottom. Maybe I need to set up a Runner's Anonymous group for those who just can't stop themselves running even when one leg is falling off. My name is Jo and I'm a Runner ...

How to manage interruptions for injury and illness is probably one of the most important things to learn as a Masters runner. And perhaps one of the hardest too.

The first step is to recognise when there is a problem. Then stop (sometimes this means literally stop now) and do something about it. No one likes to stop mid-run, but for both injuries and illness it is almost always better to stop than to carry on – especially if you are in significant pain or feel very unwell.

The second stage where many runners need more support is how to manage the return to running. Often this depends on the severity of the illness or injury and the length of interruption to your running. Jumping straight back in where you left off is often why some runners get stuck in a cycle of boom and bust. So here are the key things to consider.

Interruptions Due to Injury

Most running injuries arise when tissues are not strong enough to absorb the training load or there is insufficient rest and recovery between training loads. There are a number of common running injuries seen in Masters runners.

Seek Professional Advice

If you start to feel pain when you run then it is very important to stop and seek professional advice as soon as you can. Do not just 'run through' the pain and hope that it will go away.

Common Running Injuries

Condition	Description
Plantar fasciitis	Foot pain usually in heel or arch of foot
Posterior tibialis tendonitis	Pain in inner ankle usually behind medial malleus bone and may lead to collapsed arch
Achilles tendonitis	Inflammation or damage to the Achilles tendon, which attaches calf muscles to heel
Shin splints	Generic term for pain in shin, which may be muscular, tendon or potentially bone
Calf strains	Usually in one of two main muscles in calf soleus and gastrocnemius
Runner's knee	Generic term for pain in knee, usually ligaments, tendons or meniscus (cartilage)
ITB (Illio tibial band)	Fascial tissue on quad from hip to knee
Hamstring strain	Pain, soreness or stiffness in hamstring. Proximal hamstring tendinopathy is soreness at the top of the hamstring where it attaches to the pelvis
Piriformis syndrome	Tightness and spasm in the piriformis muscle in glutes
Lower back pain	This may be related to tightness in the lower back, hips and/or hamstrings
Stress fractures	Tiny hairline fractures in the bone from repeated overuse, poor bone density, low energy availability and hormonal disruption. Commonly found in the metatarsals, navicular or tibia. Occasionally in the femur and pelvis

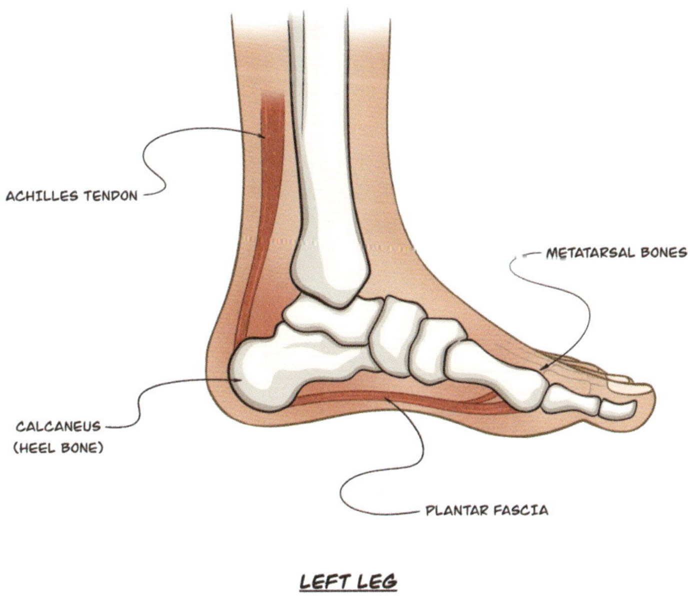

Foot (side view) showing plantar fascia and achilles tendon

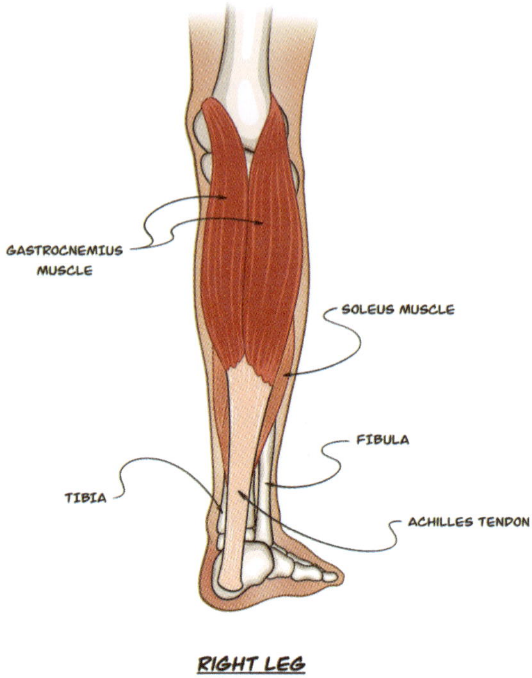

Calf (rear view) showing gastrocnemius and soleus

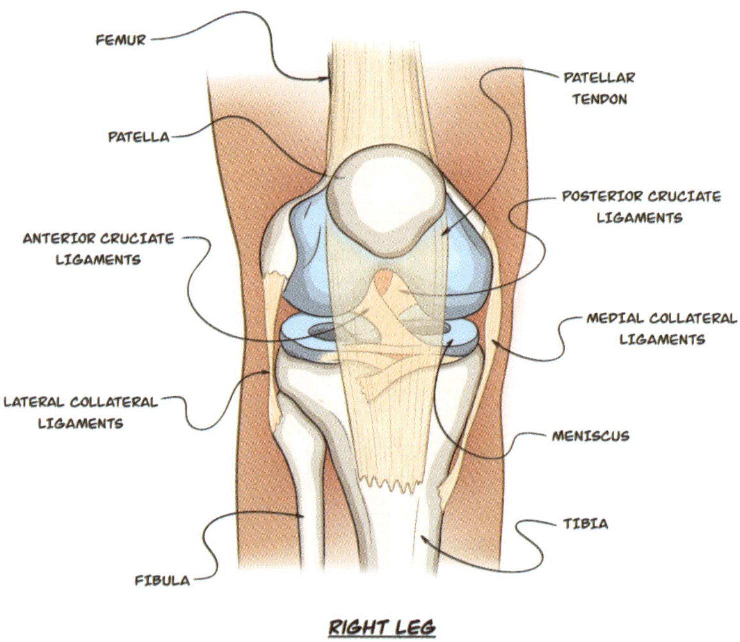

Knee (front view) showing meniscus, anterior and posterior cruciate ligaments, Lateral and Medial collateral ligaments and patella tendon

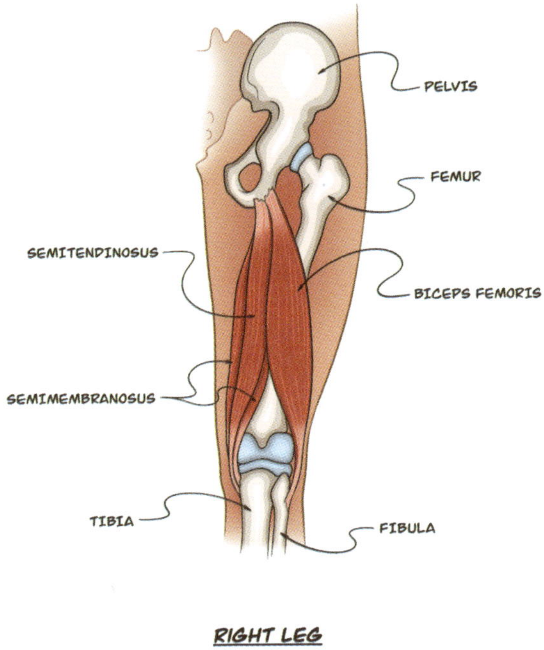

Upper leg (rear view) showing hamstring namely biceps femoris, semimembranosus and semitendinosus

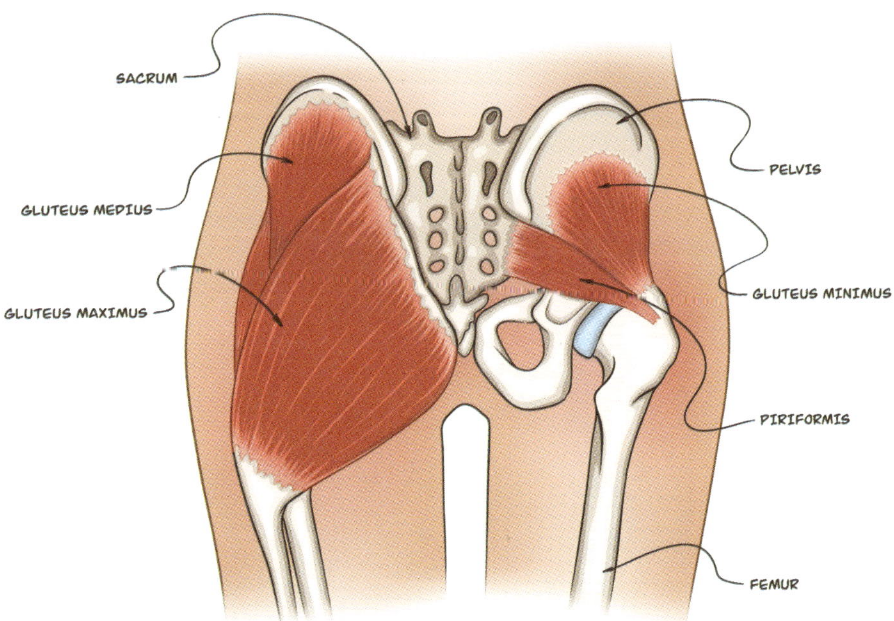

Glutes (rear view) showing glute minimus, glute maximus, glute medius and piriformis

If repeated running has caused an injury, then more running is very unlikely to resolve the problem.

Early diagnosis and identification of the potential underlying causes can significantly reduce the length of time lost to injury. Qualified professionals can advise you whether you need to rest or how to modify your training programme, provide a rehabilitation programme and a realistic timetable for recovery.

Avoid the temptation to seek advice from other runners. Whilst they may offer valuable moral and emotional support, unless they are also qualified physiotherapists they are not qualified to diagnose or advise on injuries, even if they have experienced very similar symptoms.

Rest

If you are injured it is very important to allow your body time to recover. Rest, good nutrition, effective fuelling, sleep, reducing stress and focusing on your mental well-being will all help injuries to heal.

Unfortunately, the repair of damaged tissues is a biological process and there is no quick-fix remedy. However, you can do lots of things that hinder the process. These include running and continuing to stress the injured area by inappropriate cross training or other activities.

In general these are the accepted minimum timescales for recovery:

- Soft tissue injuries (muscle, tendon, ligament): approx. 7–28 days

> *I have got better at realising that I need to rest. But still make mistakes. When I ran parkrun I felt really good but I probably shouldn't have run because I had a little niggle. Afterwards I asked myself, 'Why didn't I miss that run?'*
>
> Sam

- Bone injuries (stress fractures, stress responses, fractures): approx. 6–12 weeks

Acknowledge your Feelings

If you are a runner then running is important to you. It may be the foundation for most of your friendships and the source of your social life. It probably helps you to deal with stress and makes you feel good. It's not surprising then to experience a sense of frustration, despair, helplessness and loss when you are injured.

It is healthy to acknowledge these feelings, but do not allow them to overwhelm you. It's important to regain some sense of control by making positive decisions, setting some realistic timescales and taking proactive steps to promote recovery and rehabilitation.

Rehabilitation and Return to Running

After rest (if required) the next step is a rehabilitation programme to strengthen the damaged tissues and address any underlying weaknesses that may have contributed to the injury. Ideally a qualified professional should be able to advise you on appropriate rehabilitation required, alongside the more general strength work recommended in this book.

The timescale for return to full training depends mostly on the nature of the injury and the length of the break. As a coach, I find it helpful to break the stages of injury and return to running into three distinct phases: recovery, rehabilitation and training.

It is tempting to think of the return to running as a return to training. However, this initial period should be seen as part of rehabilitation where the goal is to reintroduce running gradually to reload the injured tissues, not to build fitness.

For muscular and soft tissue injuries, it is generally recommended that your return to your running programme should last about half the duration of the time spent not running. For example, if you missed one week, you should allocate three to four days for your return to running rehabilitation programme. If you were injured for six weeks, you may need to spend three or four weeks on your return to running programme.

Bone stress injuries require a more conservative and incremental re-loading programme and should always be guided by professional advice.

I see other runners going for five- or six-mile test runs after they have been injured! That is way too much but unfortunately most people don't realise that.

Sam

Interruptions Due to Illness

Many runners find it more difficult to judge whether they should run or rest when they have minor illnesses. When you are unwell, it is important to remember that your body is already under additional stress. As a result, it is less capable of making desired training adaptations. This means that even if you run, you are unlikely to fully benefit from the training, and may potentially prolong the recovery period.

If you have minor symptoms of a cough or cold then you may be able to continue with easy runs. However, it's advisable not to stress your body by doing interval sessions or harder runs. If you feel worse during or after your run, then rest.

If you have a temperature, shivers, sweats or feel unusually fatigued, you should always rest until these symptoms subside. If you have Covid or flu you are very strongly advised to rest even if you have only minor symptoms. It is potentially very dangerous to exercise whilst suffering from a viral infection. This has been associated with potentially serious heart conditions and may increase the likelihood of post-viral syndromes such as chronic fatigue or long Covid.

For any other serious or chronic health conditions, especially any heart conditions, always seek professional medical advice about what exercise may be appropriate.

Return to Running After Illness

As with interruptions due to injury, you should not jump straight back into training after illness. It's important, especially after viral infections, to ensure that you are fully recovered or you risk prolonging your illness as well as creating more serious health complications. Your return to running should be graduated and subject to any reoccurrence of symptoms.

Return to Running Plans

Each Return to Running plan aims to get you back to 30 minutes continuous running. For most runners after this point if your injury or illness was minor you can then return to your usual training plan.

If your injury or illness was more serious and you needed longer than three or four weeks break you are strongly advised to follow one of the Bridging into Sessions plans in Chapter 11 before resuming your usual training.

Other Interruptions

For Masters runners there may be many other reasons for interruptions to training, such as work, family commitments and holidays. Short interruptions of less than two or three weeks usually mean you can get straight back into running. For longer than three or four weeks, I would usually advise that you build up over the first week. More than two or three months out probably requires a more conservative return.

> *Before I learnt better I used to get injured, have a week off, then get straight back into it and push myself too hard again and have to have another week off.*
>
> John

Guidelines for Return to Running

- Follow any professional or medical advice.
- Ensure you are pain-free (after injury) or the symptoms of your illness have subsided before resuming running.
- After injury, if pain increases during or after your run then either repeat the current step, go back one or two steps or take an extra rest day until pain subsides again. If the pain continues then seek further professional advice.
- After illness, if you start to feel unwell during or after your run, or your symptoms return, then take further rest days until the symptoms subside, and if necessary seek further medical advice.
- Don't be fixed on any set timescale for return to running. Be guided by any symptoms of injury or illness and accept it may take longer than initially hoped to return.

Cross Training as an Alternative

Cross training can be highly effective for Masters runners. It can enable you to add more training into your week whilst managing the load on your body – legs in particular – and minimising further interruptions from injury from too much

Three-Step Plan

Suitable for short interruptions (usually 3–7 days), minor soft tissue injuries and minor illnesses

Step	Run
1	10–15min easy run
2	15–20min easy run
3	20–30min easy run

Seven-Step Plan

Suitable for short- to medium-length interruptions (usually 7–14 days), soft tissue injuries that require some rehabilitation and minor illnesses or viral infections

Step	Run
1	3 × 2min easy run (with 1 min walk)
2	3 × 3min easy run (with 1 min walk)
3	5 × 3min easy run (with 1 min walk)
4	4 × 5min easy run (with 1 min walk)
5	2 × 10min easy run (with 1 min walk)
6	20min easy run
7	30min easy run

Twelve-Step Plan

Suitable for medium to longer interruptions (usually more than two weeks), soft tissue injuries and may be suitable for some bone stress injuries (subject to professional advice)

Step	Run
1	4 × 1 min easy run (1 min walk)
2	3 × 2min easy run (with 1 min walk)
3	3 × 3min easy run (with 1 min walk)
4	4 × 3min easy run (with 1 min walk)
5	4 × 4min easy run (with 1 min walk)
6	4 × 5min easy run (with 1 min walk)
7	2 × 8min easy run (with 1 min walk)
8	2 × 10min easy run (with 1 min walk)
9	15min easy run
10	20min easy run
11	25min easy run
12	30min easy run

running. It can also be a good way to maintain fitness during any interruptions due to injury, subject to some important considerations.

What is Cross Training?

Cross training is any kind of training that is not running. There are countless ways to cross train. Elliptical, bike (road or indoor bike such as spin, watt bike or turbo), rowing, aqua jogging or swimming. There are advantages and disadvantages to each one. To get the most from your cross training you need to choose the right type for you.

The choice of what kind of cross training to do comes down to three key considerations:

- Effectiveness – what training benefit will you get from it and can you work at the required intensity to get the training benefits you are seeking?
- Convenience – do you have easy and convenient access to the equipment required.

I started adding cross training and workouts on the elliptical to my training after the first year or so as I realised it allowed my legs more time to recover but meant I could still train.

Katherine

For example, you might like swimming, but do not have time to get to your local pool?

- Personal choice – you have to enjoy or at least 'not mind' the type of cross training or you will struggle with motivation over the longer term.

Elliptical (also known as cross trainer)

The elliptical can be very good at replicating the same intensity as running. It has some weight-bearing aspect but without the damaging element of repeated impact. Cross training will work both arms and legs and the action is relatively close to running. You can also work at a range of efforts and resistance.

Indoor bike

There is a range of different types of indoor bikes. Some have resistance and some have pre-set programmes that can maintain variety and interest. You can work at a range of intensity and effort subject to the programme and preference. Many runners enjoy the music and vibe of spin classes or similar. The bike is also effective as it is non-weight-bearing, although it does put some pressure on lower limbs.

Cycling

Cycling can be a good form of cross training for many runners who like to be outdoors. You can work at your own choice of effort and intensity subject to the route and elevation you choose.

Aqua jogging

Aqua jogging is a running action usually carried out in deep water, often using a flotation belt for buoyancy. It can be helpful during injury and to manage load on legs as it is non-weight-bearing and non-impact, whilst enabling you to achieve higher heart rates.

Swimming

Swimming is non-impact, usually low-intensity activity. It does rely on swimming ability to be able to achieve a sufficient level of workout and, of course, convenient access to a pool.

Rowing machine

Rowing can be a very effective form of cross training, but does rely on greater upper body strength and an understanding of good technique that not all runners may possess.

Cross Training as Part of your Regular Weekly Training

There are two main reasons to incorporate cross training into your running training programme. Firstly, to improve fitness as an inherent part of your regular training programme. Secondly, to maintain fitness during injury and rehab.

For most Masters runners cross training can be highly effective to supplement your easy aerobic fitness without the same level of muscle damage and fatigue from running. This enables you to increase your overall training load and potentially run much faster for the same, or less weekly, volume of running.

It should be carefully planned as part of your overall training programme and should enhance training rather than detract from training. You must ensure you fuel your cross training as effectively as you would fuel additional running and allow sufficient recovery from cross training workouts.

It's also important to remember the balance between physiological fitness and biomechanical capacity. Part of the training benefit from running is conditioning and strengthening muscles, tendons and bones. and some of these positive benefits can be lost when you swap some of your running for cross training.

For most Masters runners you only need to stick to easy aerobic workouts in cross training. Whenever possible you should reserve your harder sessions for running. Cross training should be the equivalent of either an additional or replacement easy run. This could be on one of your running rest days, as long as you keep one total rest day per week minimum. Or it could be your second workout as part of a double day (a double day is when you do two training sessions in one day).

Cross Training During Injury

Cross training can be very effective at maintaining fitness during periods of non-running due to injury. 'Fitness' as a very general concept starts to decline (albeit very slowly at first) after five to seven days of inactivity. Cross training allows you to slow the general loss of fitness whilst you are unable to run.

It is very important to ensure that cross training does not aggravate your injury or prolong your recovery. A physio should be able to advise you more about what type of cross training is appropriate with your injury.

During a period of injury, recovery should be the primary focus of your available energy and effective fuelling is important to promote healing. It's very important not to significantly reduce your energy intake during injury even if you are doing less training. If your injury has been exacerbated by low energy availability, then you need to consider carefully whether you would benefit more from full rest to allow your body to focus on healing, not additional training. This is particularly relevant for more serious stress fractures.

Subject to time and availability of the appropriate equipment, you can maintain good levels of fitness by replacing your usual weekly training with an equivalent mix of easy effort and harder intervals sessions in cross training. This focus on cross training as the main form of training should continue through the rehabilitation phase. This helps remove the pressure to rush your return to running. Then as you build up your running volume again you can then start to proportionally reduce the cross training.

Unfortunately, if you are unwell it is usually not advisable to cross train either, as your body needs full rest to recover most effectively.

PART III

PLANNING YOUR TRAINING

Run when you can, walk if you have to, crawl if you must; just never give up.

Dean Karnazes, ultramarathoner

9 Training Review and Planning

Putting all the pieces together to set training at the right level for you so that it builds progressively towards your goal is the challenge for all Masters runners. Overdo it and you end up injured. Don't do enough and you won't run faster. But get it right and this is where the magic happens.

How to Review Your Current Running

Any successful training plan has to start from where you are now. It sounds obvious and yet it's often the first mistake that runners make, especially as we often have a distorted view of what we actually do – forgetting the runs we miss or overlooking all the extra kilometres that get randomly added.

Review the preceding 8 weeks

The preceding eight weeks give you the most accurate assessment of your current training and fitness. However, if your last eight weeks have been unusually different or disrupted, extend your review to the previous twelve weeks.

Total weekly volume

Total weekly volume is the total amount of running you have done including easy runs, warm-up, cool-down, intervals sessions and any other running. You can measure in miles or kilometres subject to preference, but this book uses kilometres.

> *Training properly has made the biggest difference to my running. By training properly I mean doing structured training. Balancing the load throughout the week. Easy runs and recovery balanced against harder sessions has helped me to be more consistent, do more running and get much faster.*
>
> Sam

Number of runs per week

This is how many times you run per week. If this varies greatly from week to week, note the reasons why to capture an accurate record of what factors interrupt your running.

Long run

This is the length of your longest run each week. Include the average pace for each run, if known, and any conditions that affected pace such as terrain, hills or weather.

Intervals sessions or other workouts

Record any intervals sessions or other workouts and their total volume, including warm-up and cool-down.

Strength workouts

Include the number of strength workouts and list the exercises completed with weights if applicable.

Any other relevant information

This includes any injuries, niggles or illnesses along with any other relevant information such as holidays, or if this week was busier than usual at work.

Assess your consistency

You can assess your consistency by calculating your average total weekly volume, number of runs per week and long run. Do this by adding up all the values in the relevant column and divide by the number of weeks. Note the range from lowest to highest in each of these columns.

Recent race performances

List all of your races (if applicable) in the last 12 months, including finishing time and any other relevant information. This might include adverse weather that affected performance or whether you were ill or injured prior to or during the race.

Create Your Individual Training Template

The most successful Masters runners learn the importance of fitting running around the competing demands in their lives rather than fighting against them. This doesn't mean you lack commitment or focus. It means you get the best from yourself rather than getting stuck in a cycle of boom and bust from over-training followed by another bout of injury and illness.

> *With some planning ahead I can block out the time to do those two or three precious runs per week despite the long hours, long-distance travel and jet lag that comes with my job, balanced against spending time with my children and family responsibilities too. Although perhaps sometimes my wife might disagree on the family side.*
>
> Hervé

Example Training Review

Week	Total weekly volume (km)	Number of runs per week	Length of longest run (km)	Intervals sessions	Strength workouts	Any other info
1	25	5	10 Pace 5.30/km	8 × 2min reps Total 8km		Sore Achilles
2	30	5	15 Pace 5.45/km	6 × 1km Total 9km	Gym 3 sets × 6 reps Squats (30kg) Dead lifts (30kg) Hamstring bridges (bodyweight)	
3	40	6	18 Pace 5.40/km	3 × 10min Total 8km		
4	10	2	No long run			Busy week with work and family
5	35	5	18 Pace 5.30/km	30min fartlek Total 8km		
6	40	4	15 Pace 5.35/km	8 × 2min 30sec Total 8km	Gym 15 × single leg calf raises	
7	27	3	12 Pace 5.20/km			
8	32	5	15 Pace 5.40/km	3 sets 3min, 2min, 1 min Total 8km		
Average	**29.8km**	**4 runs per week**	**13.5km**			

Identify Your Available Training Time

Start by recording how much time you have available to run each day. It's important to be realistic but equally important to commit to making the time each week to stick to the plan. However, you also need to be flexible and recognise that as a busy person sometimes you will need to make last-minute changes.

If you work on a rolling shift pattern or your work or other commitments are irregular, don't be constrained by sticking to the traditional seven-day weekly plan. Your individual template can cover two, three or

Example Race Review

Date	Race	Time	Info
June	Half marathon	1:55:23	Key race. Felt good but heavy rain and muddy
October	10k	48:35	Key race. Felt strong
December	5k	26:00	Injured for 3 weeks before race
December	5k	22:01	Felt very strong
March	Half marathon	1:47:28	Key race

more weeks to reflect your personal circumstances.

Number of Runs and Strength Workouts Per Week

The number of runs per week should closely match your weekly average and should be realistic and manageable most weeks to avoid the need to constantly readjust your plan.

Remember that just because you have time to run every day it does not mean you should run every day. Extra days provide alternative options for busy weeks. It's also important to include two strength workouts in your weekly plan (even if at this stage you are new to strength workouts). Ensure that you plan a minimum of one rest day per week.

> *I started running after my dad passed away. It's always a wake-up call when you lose your parent. But I thought to myself if I made time to drive to see Dad three or four times each week when he was ill then I can make time to run now.*
>
> Katherine

Plan Long Run

Traditionally many runners do long runs on Sundays, but other than convenience there is no reason why you shouldn't pick the day that works best for you.

The length of your long run should be closely related to the average from your review. An exception would be if you have been building up the length of your long run over the last few weeks.

Plan Intervals Sessions

The next step is to identify the best days for intervals sessions. If you run more than one

> *I do my long runs on a Wednesday or Thursday as I have the most time available and it gives me more time at weekends.*
>
> Katherine

Example Training Template: Daily Available Training Time

Monday	Tuesday	Wednesday	Thursday	Friday	Saturday	Sunday
None	90min	45min	30min	60min	90min	2 hours

Example Training Template: Daily Available Training Time with Rolling Shift Pattern

Week No.	Mon	Tues	Wed	Thurs	Fri	Sat	Sun
1	Day shift No run	Day shift No run	Early shift 60min	Early shift 60min	Night shift 60min	Night shift No run. Too tired	Day off 30min max. Tired after night shift
2	Day off 90min	Day off 90min	Day off 90min	Day shift No run	Day shift No run	Early shift 60min	Early shift 60min
3	Night shift 60min	Night shift No run Too tired	Day off 30min max. Tired after night shift	Day off 90min	Day off 90min	Day off 90min	Day shift No run
4	Day shift No run	Early shift 60min	Early shift 60min	Night shift 60min	Night shift No run. Too tired	Day off 30min max. Tired after night shift	Day off 90min

Example Training Template: Daily Available Training Time and Planned Runs or Strength Workouts

Monday	Tuesday	Wednesday	Thursday	Friday	Saturday	Sunday
	90min	45min	30min	None	90min	2 hours
Rest day	Run and strength	Run	Optional run day	Strength	Run	Run

Example Training Template: Daily Available Training Time and Planned Long Run

Monday	Tuesday	Wednesday	Thursday	Friday	Saturday	Sunday
None	90min	45min	30min	None	90min	2 hours
Rest day	Run and strength	Run	Optional run day	Strength	Run	Long run

intervals session per week, these should not be on consecutive days and ideally not the day after your long run.

Note Total Weekly Volume

The total weekly volume of any new training plan should be closely related to the average from your review. There are a few exceptions to be adopted with caution:
If you have been building up your number of days per week or total weekly volume over the last eight weeks.

> If this is you then start from your most recent number of days and total weekly volume rather than your eight-week average. *Go to* Chapters 11 and 12 for more advice.

If your most recent few weeks have been interrupted due to illness or injury.

> If this is you then you may be able to go back to your previous usual total weekly volume (if this is more than your current average). However, take account of the length of the interruption and whether you are now fully recovered. For more advice *see* Chapter 8.

Calculate your Current Training Paces

Training paces represent the pace and effort that will maximise the adaptation and fitness from your training. It can be tempting to set ambitious training paces but often this only serves to compromise the quality of training rather than make you faster.

Training paces are there to guide training so they do not need to be precise. They are also not fixed and should naturally be adjusted as you progress.

There are many online pace calculators available that calculate training paces based on recent race performances. One of the best is the Jack Daniels VDOT calculator. However, if you do not have any recent race performances then here is a simple guide to get you started.

Introduction to the Training Plans

The training plans are divided into four stages:

- Building the base
- Bridging into sessions
- General components of endurance
- Event-specific training for 5k, 10k or half marathon

Example Training Template: Daily Available Training Time with planned Runs, intervals Session and strength workouts

Monday	**Tuesday**	**Wednesday**	**Thursday**	**Friday**	**Saturday**	**Sunday**
None	**90min**	**45min**	**30min**	**None**	**90min**	**2 hours**
Rest day	Intervals session and strength	Run	Optional run day	Strength	Intervals session	Long run

Guide to Training Paces

Pace description	Guidance	Example based on 5k time 25:00 (5:00/km)	Example based on 10k time 35:00 (3:30/km)
VO_2 max/3k pace	Approx. 5–10sec per km faster than 5k pace	4:50–4:55/km	3:10–3:15/km
5k pace	Approx. 5–10sec per km faster than 10k pace	5:00/km	3:20–3:25/km
10k pace	Approx. 10–15sec per km slower than 5k pace *or* 10–15sec per km faster than half marathon pace	5:10–5:15/km	3:30/km
Half marathon pace	Approx. 10–15sec per km slower than 10k pace	5:20–5:30/km	3.40–3:45/km
Threshold pace	Approx. between 10k and half marathon pace	5:15–5:20/km	3:35–3:40/km
Easy run	These should be run to feel with no set pace but ideally no faster than 1–2min per km slower than 5k pace	6:00–7:00/km	4:20–5:20/km

Each stage has a series of two- to eight-week blocks of training. Not everyone needs to follow each stage chronologically. More information about each block and how to put them together follows in each chapter. However, here is some basic guidance to get you started.

Building the base

This stage helps you to get started and gradually, but appropriately, increase your running alongside building a strong foundation in strength work. Building the base is essential for all Masters runners within their annual training plan. However, not all runners will need to start with this plan right now.

Key factors to decide if this stage is right for you now include:

- How long you have been running
- Your current total weekly volume
- Any current or long-term issues with injuries
- Timescale to your next target race

Bridging into sessions

This stage introduces faster running and intervals sessions into your training in a structured and progressive way.

Key factors to decide if this stage is right for you now include:

- Whether you currently do mostly or all easy runs
- How long you have been running and your previous experience of intervals sessions
- Any current or previous issues with injuries

General components of endurance

This stage develops all of the components that provide general endurance fitness and give you the necessary foundation for the event specific plans.
Key factors to decide if this stage is right for you now include:

- Your total weekly volume and previous experience of intervals sessions
- Your current fitness
- Timescales to your next target race

Event-specific training

This stage has eight-week training plans specifically targeted towards 5k, 10k or half marathon.

Key factors to decide if this stage is right for you now include:

Timescales to your next target race:

Guidance on Choosing Training Blocks

If your current total weekly volume is low or you want to increase how much you run

Start with *Building the Base* before moving on to *Bridging into Sessions* or *General Components of Endurance.*

If you have been running for less than six to twelve months

Start with *Building the Base* then *Bridging into Sessions* to build some basic components of running fitness and increase your total weekly volume. Then you are in a stronger position to tackle either *General Components of Endurance* or *Event-Specific Training.*

If you do lots of running but have no or limited experience of Intervals

Start with *Bridging into Sessions* before moving on to *General Components of Endurance* or *Event-Specific Training.*

If you are an experienced runner with a good total weekly volume

Start with *General Components of Endurance* or *Event-Specific Training*. You can also consider starting with *Building the Base* if you would benefit from more

1	2	3	4	5	6	7	8	9	10	11	12	13	14	15	16	17	18	19	20
Building the Base				Building the Base				General Components of Fitness				Event specific training & Race							

Do these training blocks if your current total weekly volume is low or you want to increase your running.

<table>
<tr><td>1</td><td>2</td><td>3</td><td>4</td><td>5</td><td>6</td><td>7</td><td>8</td><td>9</td><td>10</td><td>11</td><td>12</td><td>13</td><td>14</td><td>15</td><td>16</td><td>17</td><td>18</td><td>19</td><td>20</td><td>21</td><td>22</td><td>23</td><td>24</td></tr>
<tr><td colspan="4">Building the Base</td><td colspan="4">Building the Base</td><td colspan="4">Bridging into Sessions</td><td colspan="4">General Components of Fitness</td><td colspan="8">Event specific training & Race</td></tr>
</table>

Do these training blocks if you have been running less than 6–12 months.

<table>
<tr><td>1</td><td>2</td><td>3</td><td>4</td><td>5</td><td>6</td><td>7</td><td>8</td><td>9</td><td>10</td><td>11</td><td>12</td><td>13</td><td>14</td><td>15</td><td>16</td><td>17</td><td>18</td><td>19</td><td>20</td><td>21</td><td>22</td></tr>
<tr><td colspan="6">Bridging into Sessions</td><td colspan="4">General Components of Fitness</td><td colspan="4">General Components of Fitness</td><td colspan="8">Event specific training & Race</td></tr>
</table>

Do these training blocks if you have no or limited experience of intervals sessions.

focus on strength work, you have had a busy period of races or you have more than four months to your next target race.

If you are currently recovering from injury or have a long history of repeated injuries

Start with *Building the Base* followed by *Bridging into Sessions* to develop better robustness and strength and avoid further interruptions from injury.

If your target race is in less than eight weeks

Go straight to the relevant block of *Event-Specific Training.*

If you have three to four months before your target race

Start with *General Components of Endurance* then move on to *Event-Specific Training* eight weeks before your target race.

<table>
<tr><td>1</td><td>2</td><td>3</td><td>4</td><td>5</td><td>6</td><td>7</td><td>8</td><td>9</td><td>10</td><td>11</td><td>12</td><td>13</td><td>14</td><td>15</td><td>16</td><td>17</td><td>18</td><td>19</td><td>20</td></tr>
<tr><td colspan="4">Building the Base (optional)</td><td colspan="4">General Components of Fitness</td><td colspan="4">General Components of Fitness</td><td colspan="8">Event specific training & Race</td></tr>
</table>

Do these training blocks if you are an experienced runner with good weekly volume.

<table>
<tr><td>1</td><td>2</td><td>3</td><td>4</td><td>5</td><td>6</td><td>7</td><td>8</td><td>9</td><td>10</td><td>11</td><td>1
2</td><td>1
3</td><td>1
4</td><td>15</td><td>16</td><td>17</td><td>18</td><td>19</td><td>20</td><td>21</td><td>22</td></tr>
<tr><td colspan="4">Building the Base</td><td colspan="4">Building the Base</td><td colspan="2">Bridging into Sessions</td><td colspan="4">General Component s of Fitness</td><td colspan="8">Event specific training & Race</td></tr>
</table>

Do these training blocks if you are recovering from injury or have a long history of injuries.

1 2 3 4 5 6 7 8
Event specific training & Race

Do these training blocks if you have a target race within 8 weeks.

If you want to plan your training over six to twelve months

Start with one or two blocks of *Building the Base.* Add in two to four weeks of *Bridging into Sessions*, followed by *General Components of Fitness* and *Event-Specific Training* to fit with the timescales to your target race. If you have more than one target race you may wish to put two or three blocks of *Event-Specific Training* together. You should then add in a short period of rest and recovery before you start again.

If you want to develop running fitness rather than target races

Subject to your history of running (how long you have been running, your regular total weekly volume and your experience of running intervals), you can either start with *Building the Base* and *Bridging into Sessions* or you can go straight to *General Components of Endurance.* You can complete up to two or three blocks consecutively. You should then insert either one period of rest and recovery or go back to *Building the Base* before adding more blocks of *General Components of Endurance.* You can repeat this pattern for as long as you wish.

1 2 3 4	5 6 7 8	9 10 11 12	13 14 15 16 17 18 19 20
General Components of Fitness	General Components of Fitness	General Components of Fitness	Event specific training & Race

Do these training blocks if you are an experienced runner and have a target race within 3-4 months.

1 2 3 4	5 6 7 8	9 10 11 12	13 14 15 16	17 18 19 20	21 22 23 24 25 26 27 28
Building the Base	Building the Base	Bridging into Sessions	General Component s of Fitness	General Component s of Fitness	Event specific training & Race

Do these blocks if you want to plan training over 6-12 months.

1 2 3 4	5 6 7 8	9 10 11 12	13 14 15 16	17 18 19 20	21 22 23 24	25 26 27 28
Building the Base	Bridging into sessions (optional)	General Components of Fitness	General Components of Fitness	Building the Base	General Components of Fitness	General Components of Fitness

Do these blocks if you want to develop general running fitness rather than target races.

10 Building the Base

Quite possibly this is the most important chapter in this book, whether you are relatively new to running or you have been running for many years. In simple terms, this chapter tells you how to do more running and at the same time improve your strength so that you don't get injured – the two things that can make the most difference to your running.

> *I started with just running about two kilometres every evening. After a while I added another loop and another and then a bit more until after a couple of years I was running ten kilometres each time.*
>
> Sam

Building the base is a long-term project. Although she didn't realise it, Sam was diligently building her base, from which several years later she would go on to represent Great Britain Masters. Yet so often this key stage of training is overlooked as Masters runners feel like the clock is ticking. This is especially so amongst newer runners who want short-term gains or former runners who think they can jump straight back into where they left off several years before.

It's easy to get lulled into a false sense of security from initial rapid improvements in fitness. Unfortunately, without strong foundations, all too often this initial progress is followed by long periods of plateau or, worse, significant interruptions from falling into a boom-bust cycle of injury.

What is Building the Base?

Building the Base is a long-term investment in your running. The main focus of Building the Base is to increase how much running you do, build stronger foundations of aerobic

> *I went from one injury to the next injury to the next injury because there wasn't any structure or strength work in my training. It was OK when I was in my twenties. I could let it drop off, then pick it up again and be fine. But in my fifties and sixties I just couldn't do that any more.*
>
> John

endurance and improve your strength. There is a very strong correlation between total weekly volume of running and performance. To put it simply, if you do more running then you will improve your times in 5k, 10k and half marathon. However, more running also increases the risk of injury, especially for Masters runners.

Building the Base minimises the risk of injury by putting the focus on volume over intensity and prioritises easy runs over intervals sessions. This enables you to increase your total weekly volume in a safer, more effective and more sustainable way. More running is achieved by a combination of adding extra kilometres to each run, extending the long run, or adding an extra day.

Building the Base is also time to develop essential strength. One of the most common excuses for not doing strength work is lack of time, closely followed by the negative impact of muscle soreness on subsequent runs. Without the distraction of intervals sessions or races, this stage lets you fully focus on strength work to resolve weaknesses and address persistent injuries.

Taking a wider perspective, Building the Base is also the time to develop good habits to support your training, such as effective fuelling and nutrition and ensuring you balance training with rest and recovery.

> *As I did some more running and picked up a few injuries, I realised I needed to do other things too to make me more robust and prevent injuries. Running is important. But it was not just all about the running. Things such as doing strength work or Pilates or cross training were important for me too.*
>
> Katherine

When should you Incorporate Building the Base?

In running, long-term means months and years, not just weeks. Ideally, Building the Base should be a regular once- or twice-yearly part of your annual training plan that falls between four to six months before your target races. As a Masters runner this enables you to make significant long-term increases in volume, improvements in aerobic endurance, develop better running economy and build strength and robustness.

For newer runners or low volume runners (those who run less than 15 to 20 kilometres per week), you should aim to start with this stage now. For other runners there is more flexibility subject to your current weekly volume and your goals. Traditionally in track and field, Building the Base happened from October to December during the 'off period' from competition. With the growth of year-round road races, this practice has somewhat fallen by the wayside. As a result, the exact timing of this stage within the calendar year now depends on the timing of your key races.

Some Masters runners are reluctant to include this stage as they don't want to miss races during this period. However, whilst the focus is on easy runs and building strength, it does not mean you cannot race. Just don't let your races detract from the main purpose of this training block.

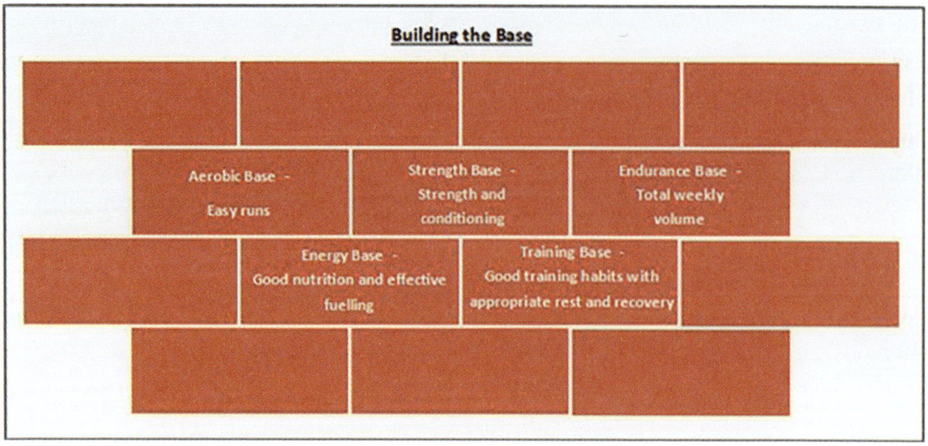

Building the Base is the time to develop the foundations of endurance and develop good training habits.

How Long is Building the Base?

A minimum of four weeks is required to allow sufficient time for your body to make initial training adaptations in aerobic endurance and improved strength in muscles and tendons. Longer periods of eight to twelve weeks bring even more benefits from greater increases in volume, as well as better development of endurance and strength.

Relatively new runners (running for less than twelve months) or low volume runners (less than 20km per week) should aim for eight to twelve weeks. Similarly, you should also spend longer on this stage if you are returning to running after a significant break.

Key Information about the Training Plans

These training plans start from 15km per week and increase to 100km per week. Start with the plan that most closely matches your current weekly volume (as identified in your training review). Adjust the standard plan to match the days in your Individual Training Template.

Each plan lasts four weeks and increases the total volume by no more than 5km for low volume runners (15–55km per week) and up to 10km for higher volume runners (60–100km per week).

Whilst these increases might seem small, they take account of both your needs as a Masters runner and timescales for adaption to both your aerobic energy system and your muscles, tendons and bones. If you double or triple your total weekly volume in no more than a few weeks you are storing up future injury problems from cumulative overload.

Minimum Total Weekly Volume

One of the most frequently asked questions is how much do you need to do to run 5k, 10k or half marathon? The answer (like the answer to many coaching questions) is that it depends.

From a purely performance and training perspective, these are the minimum weekly totals I would suggest to enable you to comfortably complete each race distance. However, the faster you want to run and the greater your ambitions, the more you will need to run.

Race distance	Minimum weekly volume	Minimum long run
5k	20km per week	10km
10k	30km per week	12km
Half marathon	40km per week	20km

For some, these minimum totals might seem quite daunting. It's worth saying that it is very possible to run 5k, 10k and even half marathons on less. However, this book focuses on how to improve your running and for most runners this does mean run more.

Equally importantly, this book encourages you to take a long perspective. So, if you are serious about your running and currently run the lower end of this range, it's worth spending the time to build your overall volume.

Maximum Total Weekly Volume

At the other end of the scale each of us has our own individual ceiling on how much we can run. The main limiting factors are:

- Biomechanical load (how much you can run before you get ill or injured)
- Energy availability (fatigue too great or inability to sufficiently fuel any additional training)
- Available time (work and family commitments do not allow any more time to train)

This means there comes a point when more is not better, especially if extra runs mean rest and recovery become compromised. It's also important not to prioritise runs over strength work either or you undermine the foundations you are seeking to build.

As you increase volume or add strength work you may notice some increase in general tiredness or minor aches and muscle soreness. If these linger for more than one week, allow your body more time to adapt by taking an extra rest day or repeating the current week of training before continuing with the plan.

If tiredness or soreness continues, or you notice other signs of overtraining, then avoid adding more.

Key signs of overtraining include:

- Increase in fatigue, which affects daily life
- Irritability
- Repeated illness or persistent injury
- Loss of appetite
- Poor sleep
- Training starts to become a chore and not fun
- Interruptions to menstrual cycle
- Lower testosterone levels

Strength Workouts

Whilst adding volume is one part of Building the Base, the other equally important part is building strength. Each training plan includes a minimum of two strength workouts per week and ideally you should aim for two to three sessions.

One workout is better than none, but progress will be slower. If you are a relatively new runner you should do a minimum of two strength workouts per week. If you are returning from injury this should be a minimum of three, with specific focus on weaknesses that led to your injury.

There is much debate on the best timing for strength workouts within your training week. However, before you optimise timing, it's more important to embed strength work as a regular part of your week. The plans start by putting strength workouts on a separate day to running, then double up as the number of running days increase. However, this can be amended to suit you and your available time.

Detailed specific information about strength workouts is set out in Chapter 3. This includes how to get started subject to your experience, what exercises to include, and how to progress.

Cross Training

Building the Base can also be an excellent time to introduce cross training into your training as long as you do not compromise the key aims of this block, namely, adding volume to your runs or including strength workouts. Cross training should be an addition and not a replacement for running in this stage and should be the same easy effort as your runs.

It's also important not to introduce too much too soon. Whilst cross training may not always be as demanding as running, it still contributes to overall training load and needs to be carefully planned into your training week. This means consciously adding more fuelling before and after workouts and planning sufficient recovery after workouts. In general, do not add more than one additional cross training session every four weeks to allow time for the body to adapt.

How to Adjust the Plans

'Sometimes the best plan is to not follow the plan' is another favourite coaching expression. It is important at times to adjust your training plan to reflect what is currently going on in your life, not just your training.

The most obvious adjustment required is when you are injured or ill. In these circumstances you should rest until you are recovered. Do not try to make up what you have missed by squeezing in extra runs or strength workouts. If the interruption is only a few days, then you can generally pick up from where you left off. For any longer interruptions *see* Chapter 8 for advice on managing interruptions for illness or injury.

Female runners may want to make adjustments to help manage symptoms of their menstrual cycle or the menopause. Many female runners feel bloated, heavy and uncomfortable during the pre-menstrual phase and it's often worth cutting back or missing these days. Symptoms should usually pass in a few days and you can then pick up where you left off. If you have a regular cycle you may be able to adjust your plan in advance for rest days at these times.

If symptoms of your menstrual cycle or the menopause significantly interrupt your training it may be worth discussing this with your doctor.

Building the Base Training Plans

15km to 20km per week (no exercises on Fridays)							
	Mon	**Tues**	**Wed**	**Thurs**	**Sat**	**Sun**	**Total**
Example Week		Easy run 5km		Easy run 5km		Easy run 5km	15km
1 Add volume to long run		Easy run 5km	Strength	Easy run 5km	Strength	Easy run 6km	16km
2 Add volume midweek		Easy run 6km	Strength	Easy run 6km	Strength	Easy run 6km	18km
3 Add volume to long run		Easy run 6km	Strength	Easy run 6km	Strength	Easy run 8km	20km
4 Consolidation week		Easy run 6km	Strength	Easy run 6km	Strength	Easy run 8km	20km

20km to 25km per week (no exercises on Fridays)							
	Mon	**Tues**	**Wed**	**Thurs**	**Sat**	**Sun**	**Total**
Example Week		Easy run 6km		Easy run 6km		Long run 8km	20km
1 Add volume to long run		Easy run 6km	Strength	Easy run 6km	Strength	Long run 10km	22km
2 Add volume midweek		Easy run 6km	Strength	Easy run 7km	Strength	Long run 10km	23km
3 Add volume midweek		Easy run 7km	Strength	Easy run 8km	Strength	Long run 10km	25km
4 Consolidation week		Easy run 7km	Strength	Easy run 8km	Strength	Long run 10km	25km

25km to 30km per week (no exercises on Fridays)							
	Mon	**Tues**	**Wed**	**Thurs**	**Sat**	**Sun**	**Total**
Example Week		Easy run 7km		Easy run 8km		Long run 10km	25km
1 Add extra day & cutback one run		Easy run 5km	Strength	Easy run 8km	Easy run 3km Strength	Long run 10km	26km
2 Add volume to long run		Easy run 5km	Strength	Easy run 8km	Easy run 3km Strength	Long run 12km	28km
3 Add volume midweek		Easy run 5km	Strength	Easy run 8km	Easy run 5km Strength	Long run 12km	30km
4 Consolidation week		Easy run 5km	Strength	Easy run 8km	Easy run 5km Strength	Long run 12km	30km

30km to 35km per week (no exercises on Fridays)							
	Mon	**Tues**	**Wed**	**Thurs**	**Sat**	**Sun**	**Total**
Example Week		Easy run 5km		Easy run 8km	Easy run 5km	Long run 12km	30km
1 Add volume midweek		Easy run 6km	Strength	Easy run 8km	Easy run 5km Strength	Long run 12km	31km
2 Add volume to long run		Easy run 6km	Strength	Easy run 8km	Easy run 5km Strength	Long run 14km	33km
3 Add volume midweek		Easy run 8km	Strength	Easy run 8km	Easy run 5km Strength	Long run 14km	35km
4 Consolidation week		Easy run 8km	Strength	Easy run 8km	Easy run 5km Strength	Long run 14km	35km

35km to 40km per week (no exercises on Fridays)							
	Mon	**Tues**	**Wed**	**Thurs**	**Sat**	**Sun**	**Total**
Example Week		Easy run 8km		Easy run 8km	Easy run 5km	Long run 14km	35km
1 Add volume midweek		Easy run 8km	Strength	Easy run 10km	Easy run 5km Strength	Long run 14km	37km
2 Add volume to long run		Easy run 8km	Strength	Easy run 10km	Easy run 5km Strength	Long run 15km	38km
3 Add volume midweek		Easy run 8km	Strength	Easy run 10km	Easy run 7km Strength	Long run 15km	40km
4 Consolidation week		Easy run 8km	Strength	Easy run 10km	Easy run 7km Strength	Long run 15km	40km

40km to 45km per week (no exercises on Fridays)							
	Mon	**Tues**	**Wed**	**Thurs**	**Sat**	**Sun**	**Total**
Example Week		Easy run 8km		Easy run 10km	Easy run 7km	Long run 15km	40km
1 Add extra day and cut back one run	Strength	Easy run 8km	Easy run 3km	Easy run 10km	Easy run 6km Strength	Long run 15km	42km
2 Add volume to long run	Strength	Easy run 8km	Easy run 3km	Easy run 10km	Easy run 6km Strength	Long run 16km	43km
3 Add volume midweek	Strength	Easy run 8km	Easy run 5km	Easy run 10km	Easy run 6km Strength	Long run 16km	45km
4 Consolidation week	Strength	Easy run 8km	Easy run 5km	Easy run 10km	Easy run 6km Strength	Long run 16km	45km

45km to 50km per week (no exercises on Fridays)							
	Mon	**Tues**	**Wed**	**Thurs**	**Sat**	**Sun**	**Total**
Example Week		Easy run 8km	Easy run 5km	Easy run 10km	Easy run 6km	Long run 16km	45km
1 Add volume midweek	Strength	Easy run 10km	Easy run 5km	Easy run 10km	Easy run 6km Strength	Long run 16km	47km
2 Add volume to long run	Strength	Easy run 10km	Easy run 5km	Easy run 10km	Easy run 6km Strength	Long run 18km	49km
3 Add volume midweek	Strength	Easy run 10km	Easy run 6km	Easy run 10km	Easy run 6km Strength	Long run 18km	50km
4 Consolidation week	Strength	Easy run 10km	Easy run 6km	Easy run 10km	Easy run 6km Strength	Long run 18km	50km

50km to 55km per week (no exercises on Fridays)							
	Mon	**Tues**	**Wed**	**Thurs**	**Sat**	**Sun**	**Total**
Example Week		Easy run 10km	Easy run 6km	Easy run 10km	Easy run 6km	Long run 18km	50km
1 Add volume midweek	Strength	Easy run 10km	Easy run 6km	Easy run 12km	Easy run 6km Strength	Long run 18km	52km
2 Add volume to long run	Strength	Easy run 10km	Easy run 6km	Easy run 12km	Easy run 6km Strength	Long run 20km	54km
3 Add volume midweek	Strength	Easy run 10km	Easy run 6km	Easy run 12km	Easy run 7km Strength	Long run 20km	55km
4 Consolidation week	Strength	Easy run 10km	Easy run 6km	Easy run 12km	Easy run 7km Strength	Long run 20km	55km

55km to 60km per week (no exercises on Fridays)

	Mon	Tues	Wed	Thurs	Sat	Sun	Total
Example Week		Easy run 10km	Easy run 6km	Easy run 12km	Easy run 7km	Long run 20km	55km
1 Add volume midweek	Strength	Easy run 10km	Easy run 6km	Easy run 12km	Easy run 8km Strength	Long run 20km	56km
2 Add volume midweek	Strength	Easy run 10km	Easy run 6km	Easy run 12km	Easy run 10km Strength	Long run 20km	58km
3 Add volume midweek	Strength	Easy run 10km	Easy run 8km	Easy run 12km	Easy run 10km Strength	Long run 20km	60km
4 Consolidation week	Strength	Easy run 10km	Easy run 8km	Easy run 12km	Easy run 10km Strength	Long run 20km	60km

60km to 70km per week (no exercises on Fridays)

	Mon	Tues	Wed	Thurs	Sat	Sun	Total
Example Week		Easy run 10km	Easy run 8km	Easy run 12km	Easy run 10km	Long run 20km	60km
1 Add volume midweek	Strength	Easy run 14km	Easy run 8km	Easy run 12km	Easy run 10km Strength	Long run 20km	64km
2 Add volume to long run	Strength	Easy run 14km	Easy run 8km	Easy run 12km	Easy run 10km Strength	Long run 22km	66km
3 Add volume midweek & long run	Strength	Easy run 15km	Easy run 9km	Easy run 12km	Easy run 10km Strength	Long run 24km	70km
4 Consolidation week	Strength	Easy run 15km	Easy run 9km	Easy run 12km	Easy run 10km Strength	Long run 24km	70km

70km to 80km per week (no exercises on Fridays)							
	Mon	**Tues**	**Wed**	**Thurs**	**Sat**	**Sun**	**Total**
Example Week		Easy run 15km	Easy run 9km	Easy run 12km	Easy run 10km	Long run 24km	70km
1 Add extra day	Easy run 5km Strength	Easy run 15km	Easy run 9km	Easy run 12km	Easy run 10km Strength	Long run 24km	75km
2 Add volume midweek & long run	Easy run 5km Strength	Easy run 15km	Easy run 10km	Easy run 12km	Easy run 10km Strength	Long run 25km	77km
3 Add volume midweek	Easy run 5km Strength	Easy run 15km	Easy run 10km	Easy run 15km	Easy run 10km Strength	Long run 25km	80km
4 Consolidation week	Easy run 5km Strength	Easy run 15km	Easy run 10km	Easy run 15km	Easy run 10km Strength	Long run 25km	80km

80km to 90km per week (no exercises on Fridays)							
	Mon	**Tues**	**Wed**	**Thurs**	**Sat**	**Sun**	**Total**
Example Week	Easy run 5km	Easy run 15km	Easy run 10km	Easy run 15km	Easy run 10km	Long run 25km	80km
1 Add volume to midweek	Easy run 8km Strength	Easy run 15km	Easy run 10km	Easy run 15km	Easy run 10km Strength	Long run 25km	83km
2 Add volume midweek & long run	Easy run 10km Strength	Easy run 15km	Easy run 10km	Easy run 15km	Easy run 10km Strength	Long run 26km	86km
3 Add volume midweek	Easy run 10km Strength	Easy run 15km	Easy un 10km	Easy run 17km	Easy run 12km Strength	Long run 26km	90km
4 Consolidation week	Easy run 10km Strength	Easy run 15km	Easy run 10km	Easy run 17km	Easy run 12km Strength	Long run 26km	90km

90km to 100km per week (no exercises on Fridays)							
	Mon	**Tues**	**Wed**	**Thurs**	**Sat**	**Sun**	**Total**
Example Week	Easy run 10km	Easy run 15km	Easy run 10km	Easy run 17km	Easy run 12km	Long run 26km	90km
1 Add volume midweek	Easy run 12km Strength	Easy run 15km	Easy run 10km	Easy run 18km	Easy run 12km Strength	Long run 26km	93km
2 Add volume midweek	Easy run 12km Strength	Easy run 15km	Easy run 10km	Easy run 20km	Easy run 12km Strength	Long run 26km	95km
3 Add volume midweek	Easy run 12km Strength	Easy run 18km	Easy run 12km	Easy run 20km	Easy run 12km Strength	Long run 26km	100km
4 Consolidation week	Easy run 12km Strength	Easy run 18km	Easy run 12km	Easy run 20km	Easy run 12km Strength	Long run 26km	100km

11 Bridging into Sessions

Bridging into Sessions is another fundamentally important but frequently neglected stage of training. It provides a stepping stone between easy running and faster intervals sessions to reduce the risk of getting injured. This stage is particularly important if you are a relatively new runner or you have little or no experience of running intervals sessions or you have had time off for injury.

Traditionally many running clubs hold once or twice weekly interval sessions, which can encourage runners to jump straight into big sessions for which they are not biomechanically (or often physiologically) fit enough to manage. Unfortunately, many newer runners do not have the knowledge or expertise to adapt these sessions to suit their ability, and more experienced runners do not always set the best example, especially when coming back from injury.

What is Bridging into Sessions?

Bridging into Sessions introduces faster running in a carefully structured and managed way that allows you time to adapt and reduces your risk of injury from doing too much, too fast, too soon.

Running faster exponentially increases the impact on muscles, tendons and bones. Bridging into Sessions is important because muscles, tendons and bones have longer timescales for adaptation than metabolic energy systems.

As with Building the Base, strength work is as important as running in Bridging into Sessions. You should ensure you continue with your regular strength workouts in addition to the specific strength work recommended.

How Long is this Block?

Bridging Into Sessions is either two, four or six weeks, subject to your previous running experience and/or time off for injury.

> *I like intervals and I was quite strong and determined, so I would run as fast as I could each session, then end up injured again.*
>
> Sam

- Follow the six-week plan if you have been running for less than twelve months or you have no experience of interval sessions.
- Follow the four-week plan if you have been running for more than twelve months but you have had repeated issues with injuries or you have limited or no experience of running intervals sessions.
- Follow the two-week plan if you have been running for more than twelve months, you have not had any significant interruptions from injury and you have previous experience of running intervals sessions.

Specific Strength Work: Running Drills and Plyometrics

Before you start faster running it's important to do some specific strength work by adding running drills and plyometrics into your training. These should be twice weekly ideally before you run or alternatively added to your regular weekly strength workouts.

The aim of the specific strength work is to improve your ground contact time, strength and function of your tendons. This means focus on short, 'snappy' ground contact in the running drills alongside good posture, stability and control.

Start with five to ten minutes easy jogging to warm up, then add these drills before you complete the rest of the run. Do each drill three times over approximately 20 metres. For pogo jumps, do three sets of six jumps.

- Dribbles
- Scissor kicks
- A-skips
- Pogos

(For more information about drills, *see* Chapter 2.)

Strides and Surges

Bridging into Sessions starts with strides. These are short bursts of faster running over approximately 100 metres or 15 to 20 seconds. The focus is on how you run and it's important to remember these are not maximum sprint efforts. Aim for a comfortable,relaxed running action with good posture and technique. (More information about strides will be found in Chapter 7.)

The next step is to include surges. Surges are essentially longer strides, usually between 30 and 60 seconds, with a similar length easy jog or walk recovery between each one.

As with strides, do not focus on any specific set pace. The aim is to build physical robustness, not fitness. You should run in a relaxed, comfortable manner at a medium effort. Avoid the temptation to see blocks of surges as mini intervals sessions. (More information about surges will be found in Chapter 7.)

Introduction to Sessions

The next step is to move on to short blocks of easy fartleks and progression runs. At this stage the focus starts to gently shift from building robustness to building fitness. However, the challenge is to continue to avoid temptation to look at your watch or to push yourself to hit specific set paces.

Easy Fartleks

Easy fartleks are an excellent, low-pressure but highly effective way to develop fitness and add some faster pace running into your training. Easy fartleks should be guided by how you feel and work most effectively as unstructured blocks of running. The faster efforts should be medium to good pace rather than hard and the jog recovery should feel very comfortable. As you bridge towards intervals sessions you can increase the overall number, duration or pace of your faster pace sections.

Unfortunately, many runners lack confidence to run unstructured fartleks because of the fear of 'getting it wrong'. In fact, there is no wrong way to run an unstructured fartlek. The aim is for you to be in control and run as hard or easy or as much as feels right. It can be helpful to use your surroundings to dictate the fartlek. This might be putting more effort in uphill and running easy downhill or taking a break when you need to cross roads. If you don't have confidence to run your own unstructured fartleks, there are some structured fartleks in the plans to guide you. (More information about easy fartleks will be found in Chapter 7.)

Progression Runs

Progression runs are another excellent way to build up towards interval sessions. Much like fartleks, the pace and effort is dictated by how you feel on the day, which means you add load and build fitness at your own pace.

Progression runs are also good to bridge into sessions because they should always start at an easy pace before getting progressively faster. This means in practice it is only the final 25 to 30 per cent of the run that is hard.

Progression runs also introduce the concepts of pace judgement and discipline into your training, which is good practice for newer and less experienced runners in how to manage effort at harder intensities.

How to Adjust the Training Plans

Adjust the days in the plans to match the days available in your individual training template. Ideally do not put runs with strides, surges, easy fartleks or progression runs back-to-back to allow your body to recover from the increased pace.

There are no set distances for any easy runs or long runs. You can adjust these yourself to match your current runs and the total weekly volume identified in your training review or from your final block of Building the Base. Do not add any extra volume in this stage.

As before, if you are injured or ill then rest until you are recovered. Then, subject to the severity of symptoms and the length of the interruption, you can either pick back up or return to an earlier stage. (For advice on managing interruptions for illness or injury, *see* Chapter 8.)

Female runners may want to make adjustments to help manage symptoms of their menstrual cycle or the menopause. If you find running uncomfortable or harder than usual, then swap to an easy day or a rest day until symptoms pass.

11.5 Bridging into Sessions Training Plans

Bridging into Sessions 2-Week Plan						
Mon	**Tues**	**Wed**	**Thurs**	**Fri**	**Sat**	**Sun**
Rest *or* easy run	**Easy run plus strides** 4–5 × 100m Walk back Recovery	Rest *or* easy run	**Easy run with surges** 2–3 × 10min easy run 2 × 30–60sec surges 60sec recovery		Rest *or* easy run	**Long run**
Rest *or* easy run	**Easy run plus strides** 4–5 × 100m Walk back Recovery	Rest *or* easy run	**Easy fartlek** Warm-up 2–3 × 10min fartlek (either your choice *or* 1min medium to good effort, 90sec easy effort) 2min recovery between blocks Cooldown		Rest *or* Easy run	**Long run**

Bridging into Sessions 4-Week Plan						
Mon	**Tues**	**Wed**	**Thurs**	**Fri**	**Sat**	**Sun**
Rest *or* easy run	**Easy run plus strides** 4–5 × 100m Walk back Recovery	Rest *or* easy run	**Easy run plus strides** 4–5 × 100m walk back recovery		Rest *or* easy run	**Long run**
Rest *or* easy run	**Easy run plus strides** 4–5 × 100m Walk back Recovery	Rest *or* easy run	**Easy run with short surges** 2–3 × 10min easy run 2 × 30sec surges 60sec recovery		Rest *or* easy run	**Long run**
Rest *or* easy run	**Easy run plus strides** 4 5 × 100ms Walk back Recovery	Rest *or* easy run	**Easy run with block of surges** 10–20min easy run 5 × 60sec surges 60sec recovery 10–20min easy run		Rest *or* easy run	**Long run**
Rest *or* easy run	**Easy run plus strides** 4–5 × 100ms Walk back Recovery	Rest *or* easy run	**Easy fartlek** Warm up 2–3 × 10min fartlek (either your choice *or* 1min medium to good effort, 90sec easy effort) 2min recovery between blocks Cool down		Rest *or* easy run	**Long run**

Bridging into Sessions 6-Week Plan						
Mon	**Tues**	**Wed**	**Thurs**	**Fri**	**Sat**	**Sun**
Rest *or* easy run	**Easy run plus strides** 4–5 × 100 m Walk back recovery	Rest *or* easy run	**Easy run plus strides** 4-5 × 100m Walk back recovery		Rest *or* easy run	**Long run**
Rest *or* easy run	**Easy run plus strides** 4–5 × 100m walk back recovery	Rest *or* easy run	**Easy run with short surges** 2–3 × 10min easy run 2 × 30sec surges 60sec recovery		Rest *or* easy run	**Long run**
Rest *or* easy run	**Easy run plus strides** 4–5 × 100m Walk back recovery	Rest *or* easy run	**Easy run with block of surges** 10–20min easy run 5 × 60sec surges 60sec recovery 10–20min easy run		Rest *or* easy run	**Long run**
Rest *or* easy run	**Easy run plus strides** 4–5 × 100m Walk back recovery	Rest *or* easy run	**Easy fartlek** Warm up 2–3 × 10min fartlek (either your choice *or* 1min medium to good effort, 90sec easy effort) 2min recovery between blocks Cool down		Rest *or* easy run	**Long run**
Rest *or* easy run	**Easy run with surge** 2–3 × 10min easy run 2 × 30–60sec surges 60sec recovery	Rest *or* easy run	**Progression run** Warm up 20min progression run (each 5min getting faster) Cool down		Rest *or* easy run	**Long run**
Rest *or* easy run	**Easy run with surges** 2–3 × 10min easy run 2 × 30–60sec surges 60sec recovery	Rest *or* easy run	**Medium effort intervals** warm up 2–3 sets 3 × 2min intervals (medium effort) 1min recovery between reps 3min between sets Cool down		Rest *or* easy run	**Long run**

12 Building General Components of Endurance

This is the point when the key threads of how to run and how to train are finally all knitted together. Building the General Components of Endurance broadens your training to introduce a wide range of runs and intervals sessions into your plan for the first time.

With this range of different runs and sessions come some other new challenges: the introduction of warm-ups and cool-downs; how to pace yourself; and the need to find determination and resilience. But as Hervé says below, from this new mix of training you start to develop not only better fitness, but self-belief and confidence in yourself as a runner too.

What Are the General Components of Endurance?

The general components of endurance were introduced in Chapter 6 and include all of the key components of fitness required to run 5k, 10k and half marathon. They are:

- Aerobic endurance
- Threshold
- VO_2 max
- Specific race pace
- Strength and strength endurance

It is true that some components of endurance may be more specific to certain race distances. VO_2 max is more relevant to 5k pace, threshold is more closely related to 10k and aerobic endurance is fundamental for half marathon. But good capacity and fitness in all these components is essential to run faster and perform at your best in any event. Hence they are called the general components of endurance.

My fitness and confidence in my running comes from all the different types of workouts I run in training. Easy runs, different types of fartleks, intervals, long runs and long runs with different paces. Each one brings something different.

Hervé

The general components of endurance are developed by adding variety to your weekly training to include different types of intervals sessions, runs and workouts in your weekly training plan. Each type of run or intervals session, their purpose and key points about each one are explained in more detail in Chapter 7.

These training plans also now bring together many of the aspects of training and skills discussed earlier in this book, including how to pace yourself and the importance of discipline in training (Chapter 1) and the need to warm up and cool down appropriately (Chapter 4), alongside the introduction of running drills (Chapter 2). The development of several key mental skills including determination, resilience and building confidence is discussed in Chapter 1.

How Long is this Stage?

Building the General Components of Endurance involves a series of four-week training plans.

Ideally this stage requires a minimum of between four to eight weeks to allow sufficient timescales for adaptations in each of the components. These plans take an important long-term perspective on building fitness and the training load is designed to be sustainable over an extended period. That means there are only one or two intervals sessions per week (subject to which plan you follow) to balance training with your need for appropriate rest and recovery as a Masters runner.

If you have races in your calendar, it can be hard to resist the temptation to jump straight into event-specific training. However, the event-specific training plans have much higher training loads (with extra intervals sessions per week). This compromise on rest and recovery might be tolerable in the short term to achieve your race goals. But over time the risk of injury and overtraining grows exponentially. Furthermore the prolonged focus on certain specific aspects of endurance risks leaving you with other gaps in your fitness in the long term.

Beyond this minimum phase you can continue with this stage as long as you wish by following the series of training plans until you move on to event-specific training or alternatively go back to increasing volume in Building the Base.

How to Adjust the Plans

There are two versions of each plan. One for lower-volume runners (20km to 50km) and one for higher-volume runners (60km per week or above).

It is very important to ensure that your training plan starts from where you are now. Adjust the days to match the best days for you. Remember that you cannot put intervals sessions back to back on consecutive days or the day after your long run. Do not drop easy runs in favour of additional intervals sessions.

There is a range of distances or number of reps for each run or session. Adjust these to keep as close as possible to your current volume identified in your training review. In practice lower-volume runners should opt for the lower number of reps. Remember to include your warm-up and cool-down within your calculation of total volume for each session.

Pay close attention to the intended pace of each run. As you introduce this new range of paces and sessions into your training, discipline in effort becomes crucial to get the most from your running. If an intervals session is too long for you, too fast or has insufficient recovery, you will not be able to complete the whole session as intended and you will not get the intended training benefits. Potentially worse, you risk overtraining and being injured from working too hard.

Finally, do not skip your strength workouts in this block. Strength is a fundamental component of endurance that enables your muscles to work at the required capacity for an extended period before they become fatigued.

When to Miss Runs and Take Extra Rest Days

The secret to successful training is to recognise when it's appropriate to move or miss sessions to take an extra rest day. This is even more important in this stage as the training load is much greater with the inclusion of intervals sessions and faster running.

I've got a lot better at learning when I need to miss runs. But I'm still not perfect. A few weeks ago I did a really fast parkrun. The next day it was atrocious weather and my leg was a bit sore, but I still went for my long run because I was meeting friends. I should have slowed down but we were chatting away. Then the next day my leg was really bad and I had to take several days off. I was so annoyed with myself.

Sam

Good reasons to miss days include being unwell, injured, unusually tired or when other demands in your life take precedence. Whilst this is frustrating, it's important to accept this happens and not to play catch up. If you are short of time at the start of the week, it can be tempting to push all your runs together towards the end of the week just to get them done. However, this can be counterproductive and increase your risk of injury, if in practice it means that you run more consecutive days than usual without any break.

Female runners may want to swap harder sessions for easy runs on days when the symptoms of their menstrual cycle or menopause are disruptive. Every person is different and this is your preference.

Adding races

There are no scheduled races in these training plans. However, you can adjust the plans to include races if applicable. Races in this block should be seen as replacements for training sessions.

If the race is at the weekend, then drop the last preceding midweek intervals session. This will be either on Tuesday or Thursday, subject to whether you have one or two intervals sessions per week. Swap this session to a short easy run instead. Follow up from the race with an easy run to allow you to recover before the next intervals session.

If the race is midweek, then drop all the midweek intervals sessions for that week and swap to rest or easy runs.

Building the General Components of Endurance Training Plans

Building General Components of Endurance 3–4 days 20–50km per week Block 1						
Mon	**Tues**	**Wed**	**Thurs**	**Fri**	**Sat**	**Sun**
	5k pace road reps Warm up 3 sets 3 × 2min reps (5k pace) 1min recovery between reps 3min between sets Cool down	**Strength**	**Rest or easy run with block of surges** 10–20min easy run 5 × 1 min surges 1min recovery 10–20min easy run		**Easy run** 5–10km **Strength**	**Long run** 10–20km
	Mid-length threshold reps Warm up 4–5 × 5min threshold reps (half marathon pace) 60–90sec recovery Cool down	**Strength**	**Rest or easy run plus strides** 20–45min run 6 × 100m 1min recovery		**Easy run** 5–10km **Strength**	**Long run** 10–20km
	Blended session (threshold & VO_2 max intervals) Warm up 5–10min threshold block (half marathon pace) 2min recovery 3–6 × 2min reps (VO_2 max pace) 2min recovery between reps 3–5 × 30sec hard effort 1 min recovery Cool down	**Strength**	**Rest or easy run with block of surges** 10–20min easy run 5 × 1min surges 1min recovery 10–20min easy run		**Easy run** 5–10km **Strength**	**Long run** 10–20km
	Threshold fartlek Warm up Continuous 4–6 × 2min 30sec (10k pace) 2min 30sec (medium effort) Cool down	**Strength**	**Rest or easy run plus strides** 20–45min run 6 × 100m 60sec recovery		**Easy run** 5–10km **Strength**	**Long run** 10– 20km

Building General Components of Endurance 3–4 days 20–50km per week Block 2						
Mon	**Tues**	**Wed**	**Thurs**	**Fri**	**Sat**	**Sun**
	5k pace road reps: Warm up 3 sets 3min (5k pace) 2min (VO_2 max pace) 1min (fast) reps 1min recovery between reps 3min recovery between sets Cool down	**Strength**	**Rest or easy run with block of surges** 10–20min easy run 5 × 1min surges 1min recovery 10–20min easy run		**Easy run** 5–10km **Strength**	**Long run** 10–20km
	Long threshold blocks Warm up 2–3 × 10min threshold blocks (half marathon pace) 2min recovery Cool down	**Strength**	**Rest or easy run plus strides** 20–45min run 6 × 100m 60sec recovery		**Easy run** 5–10km **Strength**	**Long run** 10–20km
	Track session (VO_2 max) Warm up 3–5 sets 4 × 400m (VO_2 max pace) 60–75sec recovery between reps 3–4min between sets Cool down	**Strength**	**Rest or easy run with block of surges** 10–20min easy run 5 × 1min surges 1min recovery 10–20mins easy run		**Easy run** 5–10km **Strength**	**Long run** 10–20km
	Continuous hills (threshold) Warm up 20–30min continuous hills 1–2min hills (medium to good effort) same time run recovery downhill Split into two sets with additional recovery if required Cool down	**Strength**	**Rest or easy run plus strides** 20–45min run 6 × 100m 60sec recovery		**Easy run** 5–10km **Strength**	**Long run** 10–20km

Building General Components of Endurance
3–4 days 20–50km per week Block 3

Mon	Tues	Wed	Thurs	Fri	Sat	Sun
	5k pace road reps Warm up 6–10 × 2min 30sec reps (5–10k pace) 1min recovery Cool down	**Strength**	**Rest or easy run with block of surges** 10–20min easy run 5 × 1min surges 1min recovery 10–20min easy run		**Easy run** 5–10km **Strength**	**Long run** 10–20km
	Mid-length threshold reps Warm up 5–8 × 3min 30sec threshold reps (half marathon pace) 1min recovery Cool down	**Strength**	**Rest or easy run plus strides** 20–45min run 6 × 100m 60sec recovery		**Easy run** 5–10km **Strength**	**Long run** 10–20km
	Track session (5k & VO_2 max) Warm up 2–3 sets 1,000m (5k pace) 600m (VO_2 max pace) 400m (fast) 200m (fast) 90sec recovery between reps 3–4min between sets Cool down	**Strength**	**Rest or easy run with block of surges** 10–20min easy run 5 × 1min surges 1min recovery 10–20min easy run		**Easy run** 5–10km **Strength**	**Long run** 10–20km
	Continuous threshold run Warm up 20–40min (half marathon pace or slightly slower) Cool down	**Strength**	**Rest or easy run plus strides** 20–45min run 6 × 100m 60sec recovery		**Easy run** 5–10km **Strength**	**Long run** 10–20km

Building General Components of Endurance 3–4 days 20–50km per week Block 4						
Mon	**Tues**	**Wed**	**Thurs**	**Fri**	**Sat**	**Sun**
	Blended track session (threshold & VO_2 max) Warm up 3–4 laps × 200m On and off thresholds (10k pace & approx. 15–20sec slower per 200m) 2min recovery 4–6 × 600m (VO_2 max pace) 2min recovery between reps 2–4 × 200m fast 90sec recovery between reps Cool down	**Strength**	**Rest or easy run with block of surges** 10–20min easy run 5 × 1min surges 1min recovery 10–20min easy run		**Easy run** 5–10km **Strength**	**Long run** 10–20km
	Progression run Warm up 10–15min easy pace 10–15min medium pace (half marathon pace or slightly slower) 10–15min threshold pace (10k–half marathon pace) Cool down	**Strength**	**Rest or easy run plus strides** 20–45min run 6 × 100m 60sec recovery		**Easy run** 5–10km **Strength**	**Long run** 10–20km
	Pyramid sessions (threshold to VO_2 max) Warm up 1min, 2min, 3min, 4min, 5min, 4min, 3min, 2min, 1min reps (VO_2 max pace to 10k to half marathon pace and back) 90sec recovery between reps Cool down Amend pyramid size to suit ability. Either 12344321, 1234321 or 54321min	**Strength**	**Rest or easy run with block of surges** 10–20min easy run 5 x 1min surges 1min recovery 10–20min easy run		**Easy run** 5–10km **Strength**	**Long run** 10–20km
	Mid-length threshold reps Warm up 3–4 × mile reps (half marathon pace) 2min recovery Cool down	**Strength**	**Rest or easy run plus strides** 20–45min run 6 × 100m 60sec recovery		**Easy run** 5–10km **Strength**	**Long run** 10–20km

Building General Components of Endurance
5–6 days 60–100km per week Block 1

Mon	Tues	Wed	Thurs	Fri	Sat	Sun
Rest or easy run 5–10km **Strength**	**5k pace road reps** Warm up 3–4 sets 3 × 2min reps (5k pace) 1min recovery between reps 3min between sets Cool down	**Easy run** 8–15km	**Progression run** Warm up 10–20min easy pace 10–20min medium pace (half marathon pace or slightly slower) 10–20min threshold pace (10k–half marathon pace) Cool down		**Easy run** 10–15km **Strength**	**Long run** 15–25km
Rest or easy run 5–10km **Strength**	**Continuous short hills** Warm up 2–3 sets 5–10 × 30sec hills 30sec run down 3min between sets Cool down	**Easy run** 8–15km	**Threshold reps** Warm up 4–6 × 5min threshold reps (10k–half marathon pace) 60–90sec recovery Cool down		**Easy run** 10–15km **Strength**	**Long run** 15–25km
Rest or easy run 5–10km **Strength**	**Track session (5k pace)** Warm up 2–3 sets 3 × 1km reps (5k pace) 90sec recovery between reps 3–4min between sets Cool down	**Easy run** 8–15km	**Continuous threshold run** Warm up 20–40min (half marathon pace or slightly slower) Cool down		**Easy run** 10–15km **Strength**	**Long run** 15–25km
Rest or easy run 5–10km **Strength**	**Blended session (threshold & VO_2 max intervals)** Warm up 6–10min Threshold block (half marathon pace) 2min recovery 5–8 × 2min reps (VO_2 max pace) 2min recovery between reps 3–5 × 30sec hard effort 1min recovery Cool down	**Easy run** 8–15km	**Threshold fartlek** Warm up Continuous 4–6 × 2min 30sec (10k pace) 2min 30sec (medium effort) Cool down		**Easy run** 10–15km **Strength**	**Long run** 15–25km

Building General Components of Endurance 5–6 days 60–100km per week Block 2						
Mon	**Tues**	**Wed**	**Thurs**	**Fri**	**Sat**	**Sun**
Rest or easy run 5–10km **Strength**	**Blended session (threshold to VO_2 max intervals)** Warm up 10–20min threshold run (half marathon pace) 3min recovery Pyramid intervals 6min, 5min, 4min, 3min, 2min, 1min reps (10k to VO_2 max pace) 2min recovery between reps Amend to miss 6min if necessary Cool down	**Easy run** 8–15km	**Continuous hills** Warm up 20–40min continuous hills 1–2min hills (medium to good effort) Run down recovery (same time as uphill rep) Split into 2 sets with 2min rest if required. Cool down		**Easy run** 10–15km **Strength**	**Long run** 15–25km
Rest or easy run 5–10km **Strength**	**5k pace road reps** Warm up 3–4 sets 3min (5k pace) 2min (VO_2 max pace) 1min (fast) reps 1min recovery between reps 3min recovery between sets Cool down	**Easy run** 8–15km	**Long threshold blocks** Warm up 3–4 × 10min threshold blocks (half marathon pace) 2min recovery between reps Cool down		**Easy run** 10–15km **Strength**	**Long run** 15–25km
Rest or easy run 5–10km **Strength**	**5k pace intervals** Warm up 6–10 × 2min 30sec reps (5–10k pace) 1min recovery between reps Cool down	**Easy run** 8–15km	**Continuous threshold run** Warm up 20–40min threshold run (half marathon pace) Cool down		**Easy run** 10–15km **Strength**	**Long run** 15–25km
Rest or easy run 5–10km **Strength**	**Track session (VO_2 max)** Warm up 3–5 sets 4 × 400m (VO_2 max pace) 60–75sec recovery between reps 3–4mins between sets Cool down	**Easy run** 8–15km	**Mid-length threshold reps** Warm up 5–8 × 3min 30sec (10k pace) 1min recovery between reps Cool down		**Easy run** 10–5km **Strength**	**Long run** 15–25km

Building General Components of Endurance 5–6 days 60–100km per week Block 3						
Mon	**Tues**	**Wed**	**Thurs**	**Fri**	**Sat**	**Sun**
Rest or easy run 5–10km **Strength**	**5k pace road reps** Warm up 3–4 sets 2–3 × 3min reps (5k pace) 1min 30sec recovery between reps 3min between sets Cool down	**Easy run** 8–15km	**Mile reps (threshold)** Warm up 3–6 × mile reps (10k to half marathon pace) 2min recovery between reps Cool down		**Easy run** 10–15km **Strength**	**Long run** 15–25km
Rest or easy run 5–10km **Strength**	**Short hills** Warm up 3–6 sets 5 × 30sec hills (hard effort) 1min 30sec easy jog down recovery 2–3min between sets Cool down	**Easy run** 8–15km	**Long threshold blocks** Warm up 2–3 × 10–20min blocks (half marathon pace) 2–3min recovery Cool down		**Easy run** 10–15km **Strength**	**Long run** 15–25km
Rest or easy run 5–10km **Strength**	**Track session (5k and VO_2 max)** Warm up 2–3 sets 1,000m (5k pace) 600m (VO_2 max pace) 400m (fast) 200m (fast) 90sec recovery between reps 3–4min between sets Cool down	**Easy run** 8–15km	**Threshold fartlek:** Warm up Continuous 4–6 × 2min 30sec (10k pace) 2min 30sec (medium effort) Cool down		**Easy run** 10–15km **Strength**	**Long run** 15–25km
Rest or easy run 5–10km **Strength**	**Pyramid sessions (threshold to VO_2 max)** Warm up 1min, 2min, 3min, 4min, 5min, 6min, 5min, 4min, 3min, 2min, 1min reps (VO_2 max pace to 10k to half marathon pace and back) 90sec recovery between reps Cool down Amend pyramid size to suit ability. Either 123454321min or 1234321min	**Easy run** 8–15km	**Threshold plus surges** Warm up 10–20min threshold block (half marathon pace) 5–8 × 60sec surges (medium to good pace) 90sec recovery 10–20min threshold block as above Cool down		**Easy run** 10–15km **Strength**	**Long run** 15–25km

Building General Components of Endurance
5–6 days 60–100km per week Block 4

Mon	Tues	Wed	Thurs	Fri	Sat	Sun
Rest or easy run 5–10km **Strength**	**5k–10k pace road reps** Warm up 5–8 × 3min 30sec reps (5k to 10k pace) 90sec recovery between reps Cool down	**Easy run** 8–5km	**Threshold fartlek** Warm up Continuous run 3–6 × 1km (10k–half marathon pace) 1km (medium effort) Cool down		**Easy run** 10–15km **Strength**	**Long run** 15–25km
Rest or easy run 5–10km **Strength**	**Blended track session (threshold and VO_2 max)** Warm up 3–5 laps × 200m On and off thresholds (10k pace & approx. 15–20sec slower per 200m) 2min recovery 4–8 × 600m (VO_2 max pace) 2min recovery between reps 2–4 × 200m fast 90sec recovery between reps Cool down	**Easy run** 8–15km	**Progression run** Warm up 10–20min easy pace 10–20min medium pace (half marathon pace or slightly slower) 10–20min threshold pace (10k–half marathon pace) Cool down		**Easy run** 10–5km **Strength**	**Long run** 15–25km
Rest or easy run 5–10km **Strength**	**Short and long hills** Warm up 4–8 × 2min hills 3–4min easy jog down recovery 4–8 × 30sec hills 90sec to 2min easy jog down recovery Cool down	**Easy run** 8–15km	**Mid-length threshold reps** Warm up 4–6 × 5min threshold reps (10k to half marathon pace) 60–90sec recovery between reps Cool down		**Easy run** 10–15km **Strength**	**Long run** 15–25km
Rest or easy run 5–10km **Strength**	**Short road reps (5k to VO_2 max)** Warm up 3–4 sets 4–5 × 1min 30sec reps (VO_2 max to 5k pace) 1min recovery between reps 3–4min between sets Cool down	**Easy run** 8–15km	**Continuous threshold run** Warm up 20–40min threshold run (half marathon pace) Cool down		**Easy run** 10–15km **Strength**	**Long run** 15–25km

Always seek professional advice at the first sign of any injury and stop running if you have any ongoing pain or soreness.

EGDON HEATH
HARRIERS
POOLE ATHLETIC CLUB
64
114

PART IV

PLANNING RACES

Progress is rarely a straight line. There are always bumps in the road, but you can make the choice to keep looking ahead.

Kara Goucher, US Olympian and World Championship medallist

13 Planning and Preparing for Races

Maybe you thrive on competition and love the sense of challenge. Maybe you have ambitions to run fast times or maybe you just love being part of a team. Whatever your motivation, races can bring an extra dimension to your running.

But alongside the positives come some aspects that put some runners off: lack of confidence, pre-race nerves and fear of failure. But if this is you, then be reassured that with practice you can overcome these unpleasant emotions and learn how to get the best from yourself too.

Planning Races

For most runners the main reason to race is to test your fitness and measure your progress. Some races lend themselves to fast times more than others. These are usually on a good surface (road, not gravel, grass or trails) with minimal hills. You can identify faster races by reviewing the course profile and looking at past results.

It doesn't just have to be about times. Finishing a race is intrinsically rewarding in itself and provides motivation and focus for your training. Some races are more about fun or

Races make you step outside of your comfort zone. But they also show you how much you have improved too. You might feel nervous and think 'what am I doing here'. Then when the race starts you surprise yourself. At the end everyone says 'Well done' and congratulates each other and you feel amazing!

Katherine

I trained for the Brighton Marathon in 2012 but didn't run because I didn't have the confidence and didn't think I could finish it. I went to watch with my kids instead and I remember one of the school mums saying to me, 'Why aren't you running? You were the one who inspired us to start running.' So next year I did run it and afterwards I was really ecstatic. Then I went back the next year and ran it even faster.

Sam

> *I like to be competitive, push myself and run fast. I know I do that best in races. I am competitive with myself more than other people and I want to beat my best time. But other people push me on too because if someone is better than me, I try to keep up with them as long as possible.*
>
> Sam

friendly competition between teams and clubs. If you are more competitive you might be motivated by winning medals, prize money or other outcomes such as the opportunity to represent your country in international Masters competitions. These races challenge you to race against other runners, not just the clock.

It's good practice to plan an additional race approximately three to six weeks prior to your main target race. These races build your experience in timing pre-race nutrition, warm-up routines, managing nerves, practising pacing strategies and testing tactical approaches. Other races also provide an extra training stimulus by simulating race pace in race conditions, which cannot be fully replicated in training. However, beware of entering too many

Planning Other Races

Target race	Shorter races	Longer races	Same distance
5k	Develops better speed but shorter races can be hard to find. Possible race distances: 1 mile or 3km	Develops better endurance to sustain 5k race pace. Strongly advised if you lack endurance. Less beneficial if you are a low-volume runner and have not run 10k before. Possible race distances: 5 miles or 10k	Develops specific 5k experience. Helpful for all runners
10k	Develops better speed and pace. Possible race distances: 5k	Develops better endurance but may be too tiring within short time period. Generally not advised unless your total weekly training volume is higher and your long runs are approximately 20km or longer. Possible race distances: 10 miles or half marathon	Develops specific 10k experience. Helpful for all runners but more beneficial for most to run 5k in preparation as develops more pace and less fatigue
Half marathon	Develops better speed and pace Possible race distances: 5k, 5 miles, 10k	Not generally applicable	Not generally advisable unless experienced runner with high weekly volume; half marathon requires six to eight weeks to allow sufficient time for recovery

races and losing focus in your training. Whilst races add an important dimension to event-specific training, they can also detract from developing the wider range of training you need to bring you to a peak.

The table sets out some of the main things to consider when deciding whether to run shorter, longer or the same distance as your target race.

Peaking and Tapering for Races

The biggest challenge in coaching is always how to bring runners to their optimal fitness, known as 'peaking', to run their best on the day in their target race.

Peaking successfully relies on several factors touched on in previous chapters. The first step is to build the strong foundation of aerobic endurance. The next is to develop the general components of endurance. Then work on the specific components of fitness required for each race.

But it's not just what you do but when you do it that counts just as much. Timing is one of the key factors in peaking successfully. Event-specific training plans should be progressive but realistic. Each intervals session needs to be carefully planned so that it allows time for adaptation, but does not allow fatigue to build up too much nor fitness to plateau before the race.

The final touch is the taper, the period in the final few days before the race. The art of the taper lies in the complex interplay between three components: fitness, fatigue and form. The aim is to maximise form by reducing training to minimise fatigue whilst maintaining as much fitness as possible. Get this right and it can feel like magic.

How to Taper

The length of the taper depends on your training load, level of fatigue and the importance of the race. For 5k, 10k and half marathon your taper should be between three to seven days.

Your main target race should always be preceded by a full taper. However, you would lose too much training time if you taper for every race, so other races tend to have only one- or two-day tapers. To help you decide, ask yourself if you want to be as fresh as possible for this race or do you see this race more as part of training or preparation.

General practice is to reduce the volume of training more than the frequency or intensity. This means reduce the length of each run but keep the same number of runs across the week. Changing the intensity of training during the taper period is subject to nuance. In general, it is better to cut the length or numbers of reps than reduce the pace. In contrast, many runners find it more beneficial to actually run faster than race pace in the final week to make them feel 'sharp' and ready to race. You can achieve this by swapping your usual intervals session for fast strides, surges or short intervals in the last few days before the race.

The final consideration is whether to rest or run the day before your race. This is mostly due to individual preference and it's worth practising both. Some runners feel

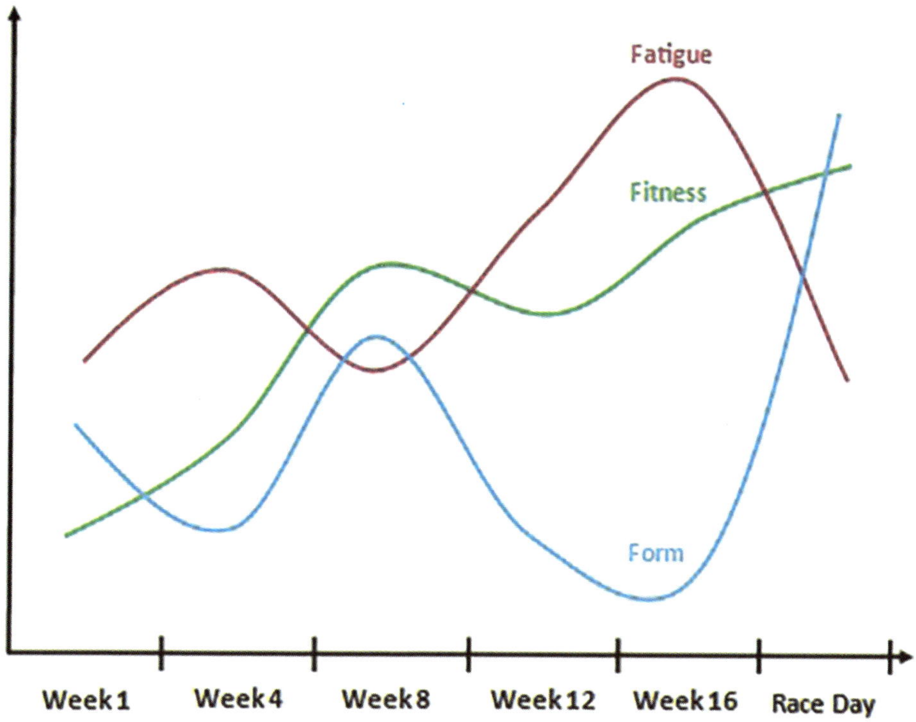

Taper is when training is reduced to minimise fatigue whilst maintaining as much fitness as possible so that the runner hits peak form for the race.

fresher with a rest day and others prefer to do a very short easy run to avoid feeling too stale. This final taper run should always be very easy and no more than two to three kilometres at most.

Target Race Pace

Pacing yourself effectively is the best way to run your fastest time. As we discussed in Chapter 1, the fastest runners tend to run even pace or negative splits. This means you need to set off with discipline at the pace you can confidently sustain for the whole race.

You can get an idea of your potential race pace from intervals sessions and training in the preceding weeks before your race alongside any other recent races you have done. Ideally you should have practised your target race pace in some of the more specific training sessions. Remember that sometimes the correlation between training race pace and actual race pace can be affected by tiredness, how specific the session was in relation to your target race and when you ran the session in relation to peak fitness.

Using official (or unofficial) pacemakers can be very helpful. But beware this can be counterproductive if you get dragged into running too fast to stay with a pacemaker or group. If the pacemaker sets off faster or slower than your target pace be prepared to run alone and have confidence in your own pace judgement. Note also that it can be very crowded around pacemakers, which can affect your ability to have an unimpeded run.

Finally your target pace needs to take account of external factors. In particular, you must be more conservative in your target pace in hot weather, especially if the temperature goes above 20°C. In these conditions you should slow your target pace by up to ten to fifteen seconds per kilometre. especially for longer races.

One of the key pieces of advice has been don't worry if you don't sleep well the night before the race. Instead I focus on the four or five days before. I try to bag all the positive energy and confidence from sleep, being hydrated, cutting coffee and alcohol consumption, and eating well. So even if I do not sleep or eat as well the day before, I know I will be ok.

Hervé

Race Preparation

Sleep

It's not uncommon to sleep poorly the night before your race. This might be due to nerves, sleeping in an unfamiliar bed or time differences if you have travelled abroad. Therefore it is more important to get several good nights' sleep in the preceding days so this does not unduly affect your performance.

A good bedtime routine in the preceding week helps:

- Go to bed on time but not early. Early nights do not necessarily help as your body clock may not be ready to sleep.
- Do something relaxing prior to bed such as take a warm bath, read or listen to relaxing music. Avoid social media and other electronics.
- Sleep in a well-ventilated, cool room.
- Avoid caffeinated drinks in the afternoon and evening.
- Do not have big meals close to bedtime.

Nutrition

It's important to eat well in the preceding days before your race and to have breakfast on race day to maximise your glycogen stores. However, you do not need to follow any excessive carbo-loading regime. Ensure that carbohydrate makes up a minimum of one-third or more of each meal and eat some additional carbohydrate-based snacks throughout the day, especially the day before. Avoid eating an excessively large carbohydrate meal the night before as this can make you feel sluggish and heavy.

Ensure you have a good, carbohydrate-based breakfast on the morning of your race even if you do not feel hungry due to nerves. Good pre-race breakfasts include porridge, toast, bagels or cereal. Take a carbohydrate snack such as an energy bar, banana or gel to the race to have approximately one hour before the race.

Note that race week is not the time to focus on weight loss. If you are on a calorie-controlled diet, do not reduce your usual energy intake to match your reduced training volume during this period.

Kit Preparation

Ensure you know what kit and shoes you are wearing on race day and that you have worn them all before. It is good practice to lay out your full kit and clothing the night before so you are not looking for items in the morning. This includes underwear, race kit (shorts, vest/T-shirt, socks), bib number, timing chip (if relevant), shoes and any outer clothing including wet weather and spare clothing. Ideally attach your bib number and any timing chip to your kit in advance to ensure you do not forget them.

Plan Travel

It is very important to fully plan your travel to the race in advance. Aim to arrive a minimum of 60 to 90 minutes before your race to allow for registration (if applicable), toilet queues, baggage drops, warm-up and assembly at the start. For big races with large numbers of participants allow additional time for congestion.

Post-Race Recovery

Your target race should always be followed by time off for physical and mental recovery. This break might last from a couple of days to a couple of weeks. Many runners do not want to miss training or races and fear losing fitness from taking time off. However, a period of rest allows the body time to repair any accumulated tissue damage and the mental break can shake off staleness, loss of motivation and reduce the risk of burnout. These benefits far outweigh any minimal loss of fitness and can be key to longevity for Masters runners.

If you have had persistent niggles and injuries, high levels of fatigue, you feel mentally tired or have lost enthusiasm, then I would strongly recommend that you take a full rest for a minimum of one week once or twice per year. This means no running or cross training, although you may do some gentle, alternative exercise.

Managing Nerves

Even the best runners get nervous. Many of the symptoms of nerves arise from adrenalin, which is released as part of

Before the Sydney Marathon I was standing in the dark in a field at 4.45am thinking 'Why am I here? What am I doing? I could be at home watching Strictly Come Dancing with a glass of wine.' Then as soon as the race started it was one of the best things I have ever done!

Katherine

our natural 'fight or flight' response, and nerves are a positive sign that you are mentally and physically ready to do your best.

Most runners find nerves almost always disappear as soon as the race starts. However, for some runners pre-race nerves can be unpleasant, overwhelming and potentially detrimental to performance. The good news is there is a range of practical and mental techniques to help you manage nerves.

Make a Practical Plan

We feel more confident when we have some sense of control and making a clear plan of timings can help you to focus on practical tasks rather than feeling nervous.

Your plan should include these key steps:

- Time to set alarm and get up
- Breakfast and pre-race snacks
- Timings and transport arrangements including means of transport and parking, if relevant. Allow some additional time for possible travel delays
- Time to start warm-up
- Time to assemble at the race start
- Allow some additional time for toilet queues

Planning time to go to the toilet before your race is very important as queues can be lengthy and this can cause a lot of anxiety, even for experienced runners. It's helpful to identify some warm-up activities you can combine with queueing for the toilet or do in start pens if queues are longer than expected. These might include mobility exercises and some running drills that can be performed on the spot to keep you moving as well as occupy your mind.

Warm-Up

A well-rehearsed and familiar warm-up routine helps you to feel in control as well as physically prepare you to run your best. Practise your race warm-up in training and other races so that you are confident in the process and timings. Work backwards from the start time and allow additional time for things such as toilet queues, baggage drops or assembly times for start pens to work out when to start your warm–up. This ensures you are not rushing it or dropping essential steps before your race.

Confidence-Building Exercises

Confidence is a belief in your own abilities and being willing to take on challenges. We often wrongly see confidence as closely linked to arrogance or lack of doubt. Being confident does not necessarily mean that

> *My best race was the Yorkshire Marathon for the England Masters Team. I had done some great long runs. I was buzzing after some good intervals sessions and I went into that race feeling confident with it in my head that I was really fit and ready.*
>
> Sam

you always believe you can achieve the outcome you seek but that you are willing to try.

One of most effective ways to build confidence is to find evidence to support your self-belief and create a sense of mastery. It's often helpful to review successful past races and training sessions and write down your strengths and what you did well on those occasions to help build your confidence now.

Runners often have a tendency to focus on what they missed or what did not go well rather than what they have achieved. But even this should not necessarily undermine confidence. Those races or sessions that did not go well, but where you persevered, are often great evidence of your determination, which is equally important in running.

Confidence is transferable. It can be helpful to remind yourself of areas of your life in which you feel more confident. Maybe you run a successful business or have a demanding job or deal with difficult family circumstances. Write down what you do well and how you feel in those circumstances. Then remind yourself you can use these strengths and qualities in your running too.

Visualisation and Positive Self-Talk

Visualisation is a highly effective technique to manage nerves and prepare for races. Ideally you should practise visualisation over time. Choose a quiet place with no distractions, close your eyes and in your mind visualise each stage of the race. Focus on how you feel and the sights and sounds around you. Practise feeling relaxed and confident in each step before and during the race.

Positive self-talk goes along with visualisation in challenging doubts and managing anxiety and nerves. When we are nervous our inner dialogue may become negative or critical. As part of visualisation, practise positive self-talk to use before and during the race to help you feel more calm and in control.

Contingency or 'What if' Planning

Often nerves are caused by fear of failure. Contingency or 'What if' planning can be an effective way to prepare for the 'worst case scenario' and is strongly advocated by leading sports psychologist Josephine Perry.

Contingency planning stops you avoiding doing things and helps you to address your biggest anxieties and fears by facing up to them in advance. This enables you to plan how to minimise these outcomes and enables you to respond in a more rational and logical manner should they materialise on the day.

Common fears might be being late and missing the start, being unable to go to the toilet before the race, going the wrong way, finishing last or running much slower than you hope.

Music or Podcasts

Setting up a pre-race playlist can be very effective to manage nerves and provide motivation. Over time you can refine your playlist to include tracks that work best for you. Some runners prefer calming music and others prefer faster beats and motivational lyrics. Other runners prefer the distraction of listening to podcasts.

Breathing Exercises and Meditation

Breathing exercises or meditation can be highly effective to manage anxiety and nerves. This can be as simple as just focusing on breathing in and out or following professional breathing and meditation programmes.

14 Event-Specific Training for 5k

It is time to think about the actual race itself, the event-specific requirements and how to focus your training to meet those demands.

The 5k requires strong aerobic endurance, balance between VO_2 max and threshold and a sprinkling of faster speed. For newer runners 5k may be more about finding sufficient endurance to finish. But as you get faster over 5k, the challenge evolves. For most Masters runners 5k pace lies between VO_2 max and their lactate threshold. This means you build up more lactate and, more so than 10k or half marathon, your legs will start to feel heavier and lungs start to burn towards the end. The 5k is about determination to keep pushing when it gets hard alongside the physical demands of running at this faster pace.

To prepare for these demands 5k-specific training focuses largely on intervals sessions at 5k race pace supported by even faster intervals sessions at VO_2 max pace. But aerobic endurance remains fundamentally important. This is developed by a good foundation of easy runs and some threshold training made up of a mix of short to medium threshold intervals and blocks of continuous threshold running.

How to Adjust the Plans

The 5k training plans are eight-week plans designed to prepare you for 5k with one preparation race midway. As with other plans in this book you should adjust the training days in the plans to match your available days.

There are two versions of each plan: one for lower-volume runners (20km to 50km) and one for higher-volume runners (60km per week or above). It's even more important not to significantly increase your total weekly volume during the event-specific plans. You should ideally aim to be running a minimum total weekly volume of 20km to 30km and build your long run up to 10km before you start any of these 5k plans.

These plans deliberately increase the training load to bring you to your peak by a combination of faster or more intervals sessions per week in comparison to the general

'I really like the shorter distance races because I know I can start faster and maintain that rhythm for 5k. And that feels really good to be able to run a bit faster.'

Hervé

Key components of event-specific training for 5k.

components of endurance plans. For the lower-volume plans the number of sessions increases from one to two per week. For the higher-volume plans there are two bigger sessions per week and some additional mixed pace runs.

As with other plans you should adjust the number of reps in each intervals session to meet your needs. In general, lower-volume runners should opt for the lower number of reps. As before, remember to include

Strength Workouts During Event-Specific Training

Regular strength workouts continue to be an important part of training. However, during these event-specific plans they must be balanced against the overall increased training load.

If time and energy start to become pressured, then consider dropping one of your regular strength workouts. However, I would strongly recommend that you aim to keep a minimum of one strength workout per week and do not drop all of your strength training apart from in the final taper week.

your warm-up and cool-down within your calculation of total volume for each session.

This training load is highly effective and should be manageable in the short term. But for most Masters runners this is too high to sustain over any extended period, so care is needed. As a result these plans also come with the important caveat that if you start to experience any niggles or signs of overtraining then you must be prepared to miss some sessions, swap to easy runs or take an extra rest day. Remember the mantra sometimes is '*less is more*'.

Planning Races

As discussed in Chapter 13, planning another race between three to six weeks prior to your target race can be important race practice and provide a very specific training stimulus. Three to six weeks is optimal as it allows enough time to recover from this race, followed by another training block before you peak for your target race.

The 5k training plans include an additional race in week 4 but the exact timing of this race can be changed to suit your individual needs and races available. To change weeks, move week 4 forwards or backwards to fit with your race date. Then shuffle all of the other weeks forwards or backwards to fill the gap.

5k Training Plans

5k Event-Specific Plan 20–50km per week						
Mon	**Tues**	**Wed**	**Thurs**	**Fri**	**Sat**	**Sun**
	5k pace road intervals Warm up 4–6 × 3min 30sec reps (5k pace) 1 min 30sec recovery between reps Cool down	**Strength**	**Threshold fartlek** Warm up 15–25min fartlek Continuous 3–5 × 2min 30sec (10k pace) 2min 30sec (medium pace) Cool down		**Rest** *or* **easy run** 5–10km **Strength**	**Long run** 10–20km
	VO$_2$ max Intervals Warm up 3 sets 4 × 400m reps (VO$_2$ max pace) 1 min recovery between reps 4min between sets Cool down	**Strength**	**5k pace long intervals** Warm up 2–3 × 1 mile reps (5k pace) 2–3mins recovery between reps Cool down		**Rest** *or* **easy run** 5–10km **Strength**	**Long run** 10–20km
	5k pace track session Warm up 2 sets 3 × 1km reps (5k pace) 90sec to 2min between reps 4min between sets Cool down	**Strength**	**Long threshold blocks:** Warm up 2 × 10–15min threshold blocks (half marathon pace) 3min recovery between blocks Cool down		**Rest** *or* **easy run** 5–10km **Strength**	**Long run** 10–20km
	5k pace intervals Warm up 3 sets 3 × 2min reps (5k pace) 1 min recovery between reps 3min between sets Cool down	**Strength**	**Easy run** 5km	*Either* **Rest** *or* **Pre-race easy run** 3–5km	*Either* **Rest** *or* **Pre-race easy run** 3–5km	**5k or 10k race**

	Post-race easy run 5–8km	**Strength**	**5k pace road intervals** Warm up 6–8 × 2min 30sec reps (5k pace) 1min recovery between reps Cool down		**Rest** *or* **easy run** 5–10km **Strength**	**Long run** 10–20km
	Blended track session (threshold, VO_2 max & speed) Warm up 1 × 1,000m Threshold rep 3min recovery 2 sets 3 × 500m (VO_2 max pace) 1min 30sec recovery between reps 3min between sets 5 × 200m (fast) 1min recovery between reps Cool down	**Strength**	**5k pace long intervals** Warm up 3–4 × 1 mile reps (5k pace) 2–3min recovery between reps Cool down		**Rest** *or* **easy run** 5–10km **Strength**	**Long run** 10–20km
	5k pace intervals Warm up 3 sets 3min, 2min, 1min reps (5k pace & faster for short intervals) 1min 30sec recovery between reps 3min between sets Cool down	**Strength**	**Threshold fartlek** Warm up 20–25min fartlek Continuous 3–5 × 2min 30sec (10k pace) 2min 30sec (medium pace) Cool down		**Rest** *or* **easy run** 5–10km **Strength**	**Long run** 10–20km
	Race week session Warm up 2 sets 2 × 2min medium to good pace reps No set pace, run to feel & don't look at watch 1min 30sec recovery between reps 3min between sets Cool down	No strength workout this week	**Easy run plus strides** 3–5km 3 × 100m strides walk back recovery	*Either* **Rest** *or* **Pre-race easy run** 3–5km	*Either* **Rest** *or* **Pre-race easy run** 3–5km	**5k Race**

5k Event-Specific Plan
60–100km per week

Mon	Tues	Wed	Thurs	Fri	Sat	Sun
Rest *or* **easy run** 10–15km **Strength**	**5k pace road intervals** Warm up 5–7 × 3min 30sec reps (5k pace) 1min 30sec recovery between reps Cool down	**Easy run** 8–15km	**Threshold fartlek** Warm up 25–30min fartlek Continuous 3–5 × 2min 30sec (10k pace) 2min 30sec (medium pace) Cool down		**Easy run** 10–15km **Strength**	**Long run** 15–25km
Rest *or* **easy run** 10–15km **Strength**	**VO_2 max intervals** Warm up 3–4 sets 4 × 400m reps (VO_2 max pace) 1min recovery between reps 4min between sets Cool down	**Easy run** 8–15km	**5k pace long intervals** Warm up 3–4 × 1 mile reps (5k pace) 2–3min recovery between reps Cool down		**Easy run** 10–15km **Strength**	**Long run** 15–25km
Rest *or* **easy run** 10–15km **Strength**	**5k pace track session** Warm up 2 sets 3–4 × 1km reps (5k pace) 90sec to 2min between reps 4min between sets Cool down	**Easy run** 8–15km	**Long threshold blocks** Warm up 2–3 × 10–15min threshold blocks (half marathon pace) 3min recovery between blocks Cool down		**Easy run** 10–15km **Strength**	**Long run** 15–25km
Rest *or* **easy run** 10–15km **Strength**	**5k pace intervals** Warm up 3 sets 3 × 2min reps (5k pace) 1min recovery between reps 3min between sets Cool down	**Easy run** 8–15km	**Easy run plus surges** 10min easy run 5 × 1min surges 1min recovery between surges 10min easy run	*Either* **Rest** *or* **Pre-race easy run** 3–5km	*Either* **Rest** *or* **Pre-race easy run** 3–5km	**5k or 10k race**

Rest *or* **easy run** 5–10km **No Strength**	**Easy run** 8–15km	**Easy run** 8–15km	**5k pace road intervals** Warm up 8–12 × 2min 30sec reps (5k pace) 1min recovery between reps Cool down		**Easy run** 10–15km **Strength**	**Long run** 15–25km
Rest *or* **easy run** 10–15km **Strength**	**Blended track session (threshold, VO_2 max & speed)** Warm up 1 × 1,600m threshold rep 3min recovery 2–3 sets 3 × 500m (VO_2 max pace) 1min 30sec recovery between reps 3min between sets 5 × 200m (fast) 1min recovery between reps Cool down	**Easy run** 8–15km	**5k pace long intervals** Warm up 3–4 × 1 mile reps (5k pace) 2–3min recovery between reps Cool down		**Easy run** 10–15km **Strength**	**Long run** 15–25km
Rest *or* **easy run** 10–15km **Strength**	**5k pace intervals** Warm up 3 sets 3min, 2min, 1min reps (5k pace & faster for short intervals) 1min 30sec recovery between reps 3min between sets Cool down	**Easy run** 8–15km	**Threshold fartlek** Warm up 25–30min fartlek Continuous 3–5 × 2min 30sec (10k pace) 2min 30sec (medium pace) Cool down		**Easy run** 10–15km **Strength**	**Long run** 15–25km
Rest *or* **easy run** 5–10km maximum Cut back run to 2/3rds of usual length No Strength workout this week	**Race week session:** Warm up 2 sets 2 × 2min medium to good pace reps No set pace, run to feel & don't look at watch 1min 30sec recovery between reps 3mins between sets Cool down	**Easy run** 5km Maximum as race week	**Easy run plus surges** 10min easy run 5 × 1min surges 1min recovery between surges 10min easy run	*Either* **Rest** *or* **Pre-race easy run** 3–5km	*Either* **Rest** *or* **Pre-race easy run** 3–5km	**5k or 10k race**

15 Event-Specific Training for 10k

The 10k shares many common factors with both 5k and half marathon but has key differences that should be taken into consideration when it comes to event-specific training.

The 10k balances the need for good running economy, threshold capacity and VO_2 max. For most runners 10k pace is around or slightly above threshold pace and requires less anaerobic capacity. However, in highly competitive races surges and fast bursts mid-race can periodically create increased lactate levels throughout the race. For all runners, the longer duration means longer focus and concentration is needed.

Easy runs and aerobic endurance are as important as ever and 10k requires a small but significant step up in weekly volume from 5k. There should be a much greater emphasis on threshold training within any 10k training plan and a good chunk of 10k race pace. These paces may be very close subject to fitness levels, threshold capacity and 10k time.

To meet all these demands, the 10k training plans incorporate regular threshold intervals with a mix of short and mid-length threshold intervals and greater focus on continuous blocks of threshold. Threshold fartleks are very effective in enhancing 10k performance particularly by maintaining the quality of the slower sections of the fartlek. Finally, speed and pace is added by some 5k and VO_2 max pace intervals sessions.

How to Adjust the Plans

The 10k training plans are eight-week plans to prepare you for 10k with one race midway to provide essential race practice and help you to be in peak form for your target race.

A good level of endurance is important for 10k, so before you start aim for a minimum of 30km per week and ideally build your long run up to 12–15km to ensure you have

---

I admit on the start line Competitive John comes out. Everybody's got a target on their back. The sad thing is though aged 68, I can't reach all of them these days especially the ones who are in their 20s or 30s but I still try!

John

---

sufficient endurance. As before, adjust the training days in the plan to match your available days from your individual training template.

There are two versions of the 10k training plan. One is for lower-volume runners (20km to 50km per week) and the other for higher-volume runners (over 60km per week). Adjust the number of reps and sets in the relevant plan to meet your usual weekly volume as identified in your training review or from your recent training.

The training plans are short-term plans designed to help you peak for your target race. To achieve this aim they increase the number of intervals sessions from one to two for all runners and increase the proportion of threshold and faster running. However, as before care is needed. Be prepared to swap some sessions to easy runs or take some additional rest days if you start to notice any niggles or signs of overtraining.

Planning Races

Each plan includes an additional race in week 4. Ideally this will be 5k or 10k. 5k races are good to include if you feel you need extra pace or speed. 10k races are more suited to those runners who need more endurance or specific race practice at 10k.

If your chosen race falls on a different week, then move week 4 to match this week and shuffle the other weeks forwards or backwards as required.

10k Training Plans

10k Event-Specific Plan 20–50km per week						
Mon	**Tues**	**Wed**	**Thurs**	**Fri**	**Sat**	**Sun**
	10k Pace Road reps Warm up 6–10 × 2min 30sec reps (10k pace) 1min recovery Cool down	**Strength**	**Long Threshold blocks** Warm up 2–3 × 10mins threshold blocks (half marathon pace) 3mins recovery between blocks Cool down		**Rest** *or* **easy run** 5–10km **Strength**	**Long run** 15–20km
	Track session (5k & VO_2 max) Warm up 2–3 sets 1,000m (5k pace) 600m (VO_2 max pace) 400m (fast) 90sec recovery between reps 3–4min between sets Cool down	**Strength**	**Threshold fartlek** Warm up 15–25min fartlek Continuous 3–5 × 2min 30sec (10k pace) 2min 30sec (medium pace) Cool down		**Rest** *or* **Easy run** 5–10km **Strength**	**Long run** 15–20km
	10k pace long intervals Warm up 3–5 × 1 mile reps (10k pace) 2min recovery between reps Cool down	**Strength**	**Continuous threshold run** Warm up 20–25min threshold run (half marathon pace) Cool down		**Rest** *or* **Easy run** 5–10km **Strength**	**Long run** 15–20km
	5k pace intervals Warm up 3 sets 3 × 2min reps (5k pace) 1min recovery between reps 3min between sets Cool down	**Strength**	**Easy run** 5km	**Rest** *or* **Pre-race easy run** 3–5km	**Rest** *or* **Pre-race easy run** 3–5km	**5k or 10k race**

	Post-race easy run 5–8km	**Strength**	**Blended intervals session (5k & half marathon pace)** Warm up 3–5 × 3min reps (5k pace) 1min 30sec recovery between reps 3–4min recovery 3–5km continuous run (half marathon pace) Cool down		**Rest** *or* **Easy run** 5–10km **Strength**	**Long run** 15–20km
	10k pace long intervals Warm up 3–6 × 1 mile reps (10k pace) Aim to add on extra mile rep 2min recovery between reps Cool down	**Strength**	**VO_2 max intervals** Warm up 2–3 sets 3 × 400m reps (VO_2 max pace) 1min recovery between reps 4min between sets Cool down		**Rest** *or* **Easy run** 5–10km **Strength**	**Long run** 15–20km
	10k pace road reps Warm up 5–8 × 3min 30sec reps (10k pace) 1min 30sec recovery between reps Cool down	**Strength**	**Threshold fartlek** Warm up 15–25min fartlek Continuous 3–5 × 2min 30sec (10k pace) 2min 30sec (medium pace) Cool down		**Rest** *or* **Easy run** 5–10km **Strength**	**Long run** 15–20km
	Race week session: Warm up 2 sets 2 × 2min medium to good pace reps Not set pace, run to feel & don't look at watch 1min 30sec recovery between reps 3min between sets Cool down	No strength workout this week	**Easy run** 5km	**Rest** *or* **Pre-race easy run** 3–5km	**Rest** *or* **Pre-race easy run** 2–3km	**10k race**

Key components of event-specific training for 10k.

**10k Event-Specific Plan
60–100km per week**

Mon	Tues	Wed	Thurs	Fri	Sat	Sun
Rest *or* **Easy run** 10–15km **Strength**	**10k pace road reps** Warm up 8–12 × 2min 30sec reps (10k pace) 1min recovery Cool down	**Easy run** 8–15km	**Long threshold blocks** Warm up 3–4 × 10min threshold blocks (half marathon pace) 3min recovery between blocks Cool down		**Easy run** 10–15km **Strength**	**Long run** 15–25km
Rest *or* **Easy run** 10–15km **Strength**	**Track session (5k & VO_2 max)** Warm up 3 sets 1,000m (5k pace) 600m (VO_2 max pace) 400m (fast) 90sec recovery between reps 3–4min between sets Cool down	**Easy run** 8–15km	**Threshold fartlek** Warm up 20–30min fartlek Continuous 4–6 × 2min 30sec (10k pace) 2min 30sec (medium pace) Cool down		**Easy run** 10–15km **Strength**	**Long run** 15–25km
Rest *or* **Easy run** 10–15km **Strength**	**10k pace long intervals** Warm up 4–6 × 1 mile reps (10k pace) 2min recovery between reps Cool down	**Easy run** 8–15km	**Continuous threshold run** Warm up 20–30mins threshold run (half marathon) Cool down		**Easy run** 10–15km **Strength**	**Long run** 15–25km
Rest *or* **Easy run** 10–15km **Strength**	**5k pace intervals** Warm up 3 sets 3 × 2min reps (5k pace) 1min recovery between reps 3min between sets Cool down	**Easy run** 8–15km	**Easy run with block of surges** 10–20min easy run 5 × 1min surges 1min recovery 10–20min easy run	**Rest** *or* **Pre-race easy run** 3–5km	**Rest** *or* **Pre-race easy run** 2–3km	**5k or 10k race**

Rest *or* **Easy run** 5–10km **No Strength**	**Easy run** 8–15km	**Easy run** 8–15km	**Blended intervals session (5k & half marathon pace)** Warm up 4–6 × 3min reps (5k pace) 1min 30sec recovery between reps 3–4min recovery 5–8km continuous run (half marathon pace) Cool down		**Easy run** 10–15km **Strength**	**Long run** 15–25km
Rest or **Easy run** 10–15km **Strength**	**10k pace long intervals** Warm up 6–8 × 1 mile reps (10k pace) Aim to add on extra mile rep. 2min recovery between reps Cool down	**Easy run** 8–15km	**VO_2 max intervals** Warm up 3–4 sets 4 × 400m reps (VO_2 max pace) 1min recovery between reps 4min between sets Cool down		**Easy run** 10–15km **Strength**	**Long run** 15–25km
Rest *or* **Easy run** 10–15km **Strength**	**10k pace road reps** Warm up 6–10 × 3min 30sec reps (10k pace) 1min 30sec recovery between reps Cool down	**Easy run** 8–15km	**Threshold fartlek** Warm up 25–35min fartlek Continuous 5–7 × 2min 30sec (10k pace) 2min 30sec (medium pace) Cool down		**Easy run** 10–15km **Strength**	**Long run** 15–25km
Rest *or* **Easy run** 5–10km Max Cut back run to 2/3rds of usual length No Strength workout this week	**Race week session** Warm up 2 sets 2 × 2min medium to good pace reps No set pace, run to feel & don't look at watch 1min 30sec recovery between reps 3min between sets Cool down	**Easy run** 5km Max as race week	**Easy run with block of surges** 10min easy run 3 × 1min surges 1min recovery 10min easy run	**Rest** *or* **Pre-race easy run** 2–3km	**Rest** *or* **Pre-race easy run** 2–3km	**10k race**

16 Event-Specific Training for Half Marathon

The half marathon is another longer event that raises some new points to consider as well as sharing many of the common elements of the 5k and 10k. For newer runners, it may well be about simply finishing the distance. But with a long-term perspective, you can direct your training to making significant improvements in times.

Good endurance and a solid aerobic base are fundamental for the half marathon and, more so than for the shorter race distances, total weekly volume needs to be robust. On top of this, strong threshold capacity and good running economy are essential. However, whilst VO_2 max plays some role in the half marathon, it has less direct relevance than for 5k to 10k.

To meet these specific demands, it's even more important to have a good weekly volume of running behind you before you focus on specific half marathon training rather than try to increase your running as you go. With this base of endurance, the half marathon training plan can then focus on lots of threshold. This is made up of threshold intervals, threshold fartleks and several longer blocks of threshold. There are some 5k pace intervals sessions to provide some pace, but no specific VO_2 max sessions in this plan.

One of the major differences between the half marathon and the 5k and 10k plans is the introduction of mixed-pace long runs. These are long runs that include some blocks of half marathon pace within the run and are highly effective training for longer distances.

Last but not least as the half marathon is a long race, pace judgement and, in particular, discipline in the early stages becomes even more important. It's easy to underestimate how much time you can haemorrhage in the latter stages if you set off too quickly. Then for all runners it's about focus and determination to get to the end.

The combination of my pace management and the conditions on the day which were absolutely perfect made it a great Half Marathon. I started the race very, very cautiously and followed the pacer. Then I was increasing pace throughout with a much better second half in terms of time and energy, which I've never managed before, meant I felt like I could have kept going!

Hervé

How to Adjust the Plans

As it's a significantly longer event, the half marathon training plans are ideally based on a minimum of 40 to 50km total weekly volume. To ensure you have the required endurance to finish the race, the long run should be a minimum of 20km before you start the plan. More competitive runners may wish to extend their long run up to 24 to 26km in preparation for half marathon training.

It's very important to acknowledge that it is more than possible to train for the half marathon on less weekly volume and

Key components of event-specific training for half marathon.

shorter long runs. However, this starts to shift your focus more towards finishing the distance than improving your time. To make significant improvements in your half marathon time you should aim to increase your base of running over the long term. More information about how to do this safely will be found in Chapter 10.

As before, adjust the training days in the plan to suit your time available as long as you do not put two sessions back-to-back or on consecutive days before or after mixed-pace long runs. There are two versions of each plan, for lower-volume runners (20–50km per week) and higher-volume runners (over 60km per week).

The increased volume of running in these plans brings a greater risk of injury and it becomes even more important to listen to your body. Stop, take an extra rest day, cut back some runs or swap some sessions to easy days if you start to pick up any niggles or notice any signs of overtiredness and overtraining.

Planning Races

The half marathon training plans include one race in week 4. Ideally this should be 5k or 10k. For most runners it is not advisable to run another half marathon before your target race as it's difficult to allow sufficient time for recovery and follow up with another training block within the eight-week timescale.

You can change the timing of this race by moving week 4 and shuffling the other weeks forwards or backwards as appropriate.

Mid-Race Nutrition

One aspect where the half marathon differs significantly from 5k or 10k is the issue of mid-race nutrition.

During running we use glycogen from the muscles for energy. The body can only store enough glycogen to fuel approximately 90 minutes of mid-intensity exercise before glycogen stores are depleted and runners have to slow down or stop.

It might seem obvious that if the half marathon lasts over 90 minutes then mid-race nutrition is necessary. However, two factors affect this. Slower pace and lower-intensity effort may delay glycogen depletion so additional fuelling is not required. Conversely, harder effort may speed up glycogen depletion, so mid-race nutrition is required sooner than 90 minutes.

The benefit of mid-race nutrition can also be affected by gastrointestinal side effects such as nausea, vomiting, cramps and diarrhoea, which will significantly hamper performance. These issues are caused by blood being diverted away from your digestive system to focus on the production of energy in the muscles. However, with practice, you can train your body to reduce these symptoms and mitigate this challenge.

However, the jury is still out on the benefits of mid-race nutrition for most runners, so it comes down to personal choice and preference along with ability to tolerate it without unpleasant side effects.

What to Eat

You should aim to have 30–60 grams of carbohydrate at roughly halfway in the race.

It is also important to drink fluids to help aid digestion and absorption. There are a range of possible options available. These are the key points to consider:

- Can you physically eat, chew and swallow it while you breathe and run?
- Do you like it?
- Can you carry it or get it on the course?
- Does it cause you gastrointestinal issues?

Energy gels are specifically designed to be high in carbohydrates and are easy and convenient to consume. However, they are heavily processed, which may cause more gastrointestinal issues. They come in a variety of flavours, textures and concentrations. It is important to sample a range of gels to see which you prefer.

Jelly babies or other similar chewy sweets can be an effective alternative. They are significantly lower in carbohydrate, so you will need to consume more for the same energy value.

Real food is often kindest to your stomach but can be trickier to carry or access mid-race. Popular options include bananas, dried fruit or cereal bars.

How to Practice

- Start practising on your long runs at least eight weeks before your target race and ideally within other races too.
- Start with smaller quantities and gradually increase as your body adapts.
- If you struggle with the sensation of having food in your stomach while you run, then practise eating small quantities before your shorter runs to help you adjust.
- Persevere. Don't be put off if at first you find it difficult or unpleasant.

Finally, remember mid-race nutrition is not essential. If you are struggling to tolerate any mid-race nutrition then it's OK to not use it. As we said at the start, there is still much debate on the benefits of mid-race nutrition for most runners in half marathon. If it proves too difficult or unpleasant then do not pursue it.

Half Marathon Mid-Race Nutrition

Product	Carbohydrate	Quantity
Energy gels	20–40g subject to brand (check product information)	1–2
Jelly babies	Approx. 3g per sweet	5–10 sweets
Banana	Approx. 30g	1
Cereal bar	Approx 30g (check product information)	1
Raisins or other dried fruit (approx. one handful)	Approx 20–30g	1–2 handfuls

Half Marathon Training Plans

Half Marathon Event-Specific Plan 30–50km per week						
Mon	**Tues**	**Wed**	**Thurs**	**Fri**	**Sat**	**Sun**
	10k pace long intervals Warm up 3–4 × 1 mile reps (10k pace) 2mins recovery between reps Cool down	**Strength**	**Easy run with surges** 2–3 x 10min easy run 2 × 30–1min surges 1min recovery		**Easy run** 5–10km **Strength**	**Long run** 20km
	Blended intervals session (5k & half marathon pace) Warm up 4–5 × 3min reps (5k pace) 1min 30sec recovery between reps 3–4min recovery 3–5km continuous run (HM pace) Cool down	**Strength**	**Easy run** 5km		**Easy run** 5-10km **Strength**	**Mixed pace long run** 20km Total 1km jog warm up 3 x 4km (easy pace) 2km (half marathon pace) 1km jog cool down
	10k pace road reps Warm up 5–8 × 3min 30sec reps (10k–half marathon pace) 1min 30sec recovery between reps Cool down	**Strength**	**Long threshold blocks** Warm up 2 × 10–15min threshold blocks (half marathon pace) 3min recovery between blocks Cool down		**Easy run** 5–10km **Strength**	**Long run** 20km
	5k pace road intervals Warm up 5–6 × 2min 30sec reps (5k pace) 1min recovery between reps Cool down	**Strength**	**Easy run** 5–8km	**Rest** *or* **Pre-race easy run** 3–5km	**Rest** *or* **Pre-race easy run** 2–3km	**5k or 10k race**

(continued overleaf)

	Easy run 5–8km Post race recovery	**Strength**	**Threshold fartlek** Warm up 15–20min fartlek Continuous 3–4 × 2min 30sec (10k pace) 2min 30sec (medium pace) Cool down		**Easy run** 5–10km **Strength**	**Mixed pace long run** 20km Total: 1km jog warm up 3 × 3km (easy pace) 3km (half marathon pace) 1km jog cool down
	Easy run with block of surges: 10–20min easy run 5 × 1min surges 1min recovery 10–20min easy run	**Strength**	**Blended intervals session (5k and half marathon pace)** Warm up 4–6 × 3min reps (5k pace) 1min 30sec recovery between reps 3–4min recovery 4–6km continuous run (half marathon pace) Cool down		**Easy run** 5–10km **Strength**	**Long run** 20km
	Mid-length threshold reps Warm up 4–5 × 5min threshold reps (half marathon pace) 60–90sec recovery Cool down	**Strength**	**Easy run** 5–8km		**Easy run** 5–10km **Strength**	**Mixed pace long run** 20km Total 1km jog warm up 2 × 5km (easy pace) 4km (half marathon pace) 1km jog cool down
	Easy run with block of surges 10–20min easy run 5 × 1min surges 1min recovery 10–20min easy run	No strength workout this week	**Easy run** 5km	**Rest** *or* **Pre-race easy run** 2–3km	**Rest** *or* **Pre-race easy run** 2–3km	**Half marathon race**

Half Marathon Training Plans

Half Marathon Event-Specific Plan 60–100km per week						
Mon	**Tues**	**Wed**	**Thurs**	**Fri**	**Sat**	**Sun**
Rest *or* **Easy run** 8–15km **Strength**	**10k pace long intervals** Warm up 4–6 × 1 mile reps (10k pace) 2min recovery between reps Cool down	**Easy run** 8–15km	**10k pace road reps** Warm up 10–15 × 2min 30sec reps (10k pace) 1min recovery Cool down		**Easy run** 10–15km **Strength**	**Long run** 20–25km
Rest *or* **Easy run** 8–15km **Strength**	**Blended intervals session (5k & half marathon pace)** Warm up 5–6 × 3min reps (5k pace) 1min 30sec recovery between reps 3–4min recovery 5–8km continuous run (half marathon pace) Cool down	**Easy run** 8–15km	**Easy run with surges** 2–3 × 10min easy run 2 × 30sec to 1min surges 1min recovery		**Easy run** 10–15km **Strength**	**Mixed pace long run** 23–25km Total 1–2km jog warm up 3 x 5km (easy pace) 2km (half marathon pace) 1–2km jog cool down
Rest *or* **Easy run** 8–15km **Strength**	**10k pace road reps** Warm up 6–10 × 3min 30sec reps (10k pace) 1min–1min 30sec (if required) recovery between reps Cool down	**Easy run** 8–15km	**Long threshold blocks** Warm up 3–4 × 10min threshold blocks (half marathon pace) 3min recovery between blocks Cool down		**Easy run** 10–15km **Strength**	**Long run** 20–25km
Rest *or* **Easy run** 8–15km **Strength**	**5k pace intervals** Warm up 3 sets 3 × 2min reps (5k pace) 1min recovery between reps 3min between sets Cool down	**Easy run** 8–15km	**Easy run with block of surges** 10min easy run 3 × 1min surges 1min recovery 10min easy run	**Rest** *or* **Pre-race easy run** 3–5km	**Rest** *or* **Pre-race easy run** 2–3km	**5k or 10k race**

(continued overleaf)

Rest *or* **Easy run** 5–10km **No Strength**	**Easy run** 8–12km	**Easy run** 8–15km	**Threshold fartlek** Warm up 30–40min fartlek Continuous 6–8 × 2min 30sec (10k pace) 2min 30sec (medium pace) Cool down		**Easy run** 10–15km **Strength**	**Mixed pace long run** 23–25km Total 1–2km jog warm up 3 × 4km (easy pace) 3km (half marathon pace) 1–2km jog cool down
Rest *or* **Easy run** 8–15km **Strength**	**Easy run with block of surges** 10min easy run 5 × 1min surges 1min recovery 10min easy run	**Easy run** 8–15km	**Blended intervals session (5k & half marathon pace)** Warm up 6 × 3min reps (5k pace) 1min 30sec recovery between reps 3–4min recovery 6–8km continuous run (half marathon pace) Cool down		**Easy run** 10–15km **Strength**	**Long run** 20–25km
Rest *or* **Easy run** 8–15km **Strength**	**Mid-length threshold reps** Warm up 6–8 × 5min threshold reps (10k to half marathon pace) 60–90sec recovery Cool down	**Easy run** 8–15km	**Easy run** 5–8km		**Easy run** 10–15km **Strength**	**Mixed pace long run** 22–24km Total 1–2km jog warm up 2 × 5km (easy pace) 5km (half marathon pace) 1–2km jog cool down
Rest *or* **Easy run** 5–10km Max Cut back run to 2/3rds of usual length No Strength workout this week	**Easy run with block of surges** 10–15min easy run 3–5 × 1min surges 1min recovery 10–15min easy run	**Easy run** 5km Max as race week	**Easy run** 5km	**Rest** *or* **Pre-race easy run** 2–3km	**Rest** or **Pre-race easy run** 2–3km	**Half marathon race**

Afterword

I started this book by saying that you are never too old to start running. The purpose of this book has been to show you how. So I wanted to leave the last words to the Masters runners I have coached over the years who have proved this to be true.

What is so good about running? Well, it doesn't take much time or equipment to get started. You only need a pair of shoes and can go out of the door for just 20 or 30 minutes. The health benefits are so clear. Climbing stairs. Losing weight and feeling fitter.

But for me it's really about the anchoring and the quietening it brings to the rest of the day. It takes away any anxiety, worry and the endless busy mind from everything else. It resets my brain into a place where I can feel peaceful and enjoy life.

Hervé

I started running to raise money for the hospice that cared for Dad. Now it makes me smile to think that through his terrible illness Dad has taken me all over the world to run. I have made friends I would never have otherwise made.

What would I be like if I hadn't started running? I think I'd look older for a start. I'd have health issues. And I wouldn't be married to my husband who I met through running either.

Of course some days everything aches. But even on the murky, grey days, once I get out of the door I feel strong and youthful and combative and ready for anything. And I think to myself 'What could be better than this!'

Katherine

Why am I still running all these years later even though I am slowing down a bit? I guess it's still the sense of achievement. Well let me give you an example. I ran the Chicago Marathon last year. It was the Masters World Age Group Marathon. I finished 23rd in my age category. I just loved being able to say, 'Hey I came 23rd in the world championship'.

So yes, the time might be slower but the sense of accomplishment is as good as ever! Now I am not wishing time away but I am looking forwards to turning 70 in two years and running the Tokyo Marathon in a new age category.

John

Running has brought so much to my life for which I am grateful. Not just health and fitness but all my friends and an amazing social life.

But recently what has inspired me most was taking part in the World Masters Championships in Gothenburg. When I went there, in my head I was thinking, I am turning 60 and probably on the downwards spiral. Then in the race I was beaten by two minutes by a 75-year-old woman. So I looked her up afterwards. She is called Jeannie Rice and has got thirteen age group world records to her name.

The whole experience changed my mindset. I thought I am not getting old. It's not time to sit down and shrivel up on the sofa. If all these people are still running really well, then so can I!

Sam

These incredible Masters runners have inspired this book and hopefully now have inspired you to see what you can achieve too.

If you want to take your running further then follow me on social media @runningjo10k or get in touch through my website www.runningjo.co.uk to find out more.

Index

First published in 2026 by
The Crowood Press Ltd
Ramsbury, Marlborough
Wiltshire SN8 2HR

enquiries@crowood.com
www.crowood.com

British Library Cataloguing-in-Publication Data
A catalogue record for this book is available from the British Library.

For product safety-related questions, contact:
productsafety@crowood.com

ISBN 978 0 7198 4623 6

Disclaimer
Performing the exercises or utilising any information contained in this book is done at your own risk. Neither the author nor the publisher shall be held liable for any injuries, health issues, or damages resulting from the use of this book. By using this book, you agree to assume full responsibility for any and all injuries or damages that may occur, and you expressly waive any claims against the author or publisher arising from your use of the information or exercises contained herein.

Typeset by Simons and Sons

Cover design by Susan Richards

Printed and bound in India by Parksons Graphics

Acknowledgements and Credits

Writing this book would not have been possible without the support of my husband David and the enthusiasm of my children Callum and Neve. Special thanks to Claire and Al for being patient and willing models; Steve for the amazing photos; Dave my strength coach for the guidance and use of the gym; Katherine, Sam, Hervé and John for sharing their stories and putting their faith in me as a coach: and finally my own coaches Alex and Rosemary without whom I would not have achieved what I did.